ROUGH GUIDES **PHRASEBOOK**

POLISH

ROUGH GUIDES

Contacting the Editors

Every effort has been made to provide accurate information in this publication, but changes are inevitable. The publisher cannot be responsible for any resulting loss, inconvenience or injury.
We would appreciate it if readers would call our attention to any errors or outdated information. We also welcome your suggestions; if you come across a relevant expression not in our phrase book, please contact us at: **mail@uk.roughguides.com**

All Rights Reserved
© 2019 APA Publications (UK) Ltd.

Cover & Interior Design: Slawomir Krajewski
Head of Production: Rebeka Davies
Production Manager: Rebecca Hancock
Picture Researcher: Slawomir Krajewski
Cover Photo: all shutterstock

Interior Photos: all shutterstock

CONTENTS

INTRODUCTION

PRACTICALITIES

ON THE WAY

LEISURE TIME

SAFE TRAVEL

FOOD

PEOPLE

DICTIONARY

PRONUNCIATION

This section is designed to familiarize you with the sounds of Polish using our simplified phonetic transcription. You'll find the pronunciation of the Polish letters and sounds explained below, together with their imitated equivalents. To use this system, found throughout the phrase book, simply read the pronunciation as if it were English, noting any special rules below.

Underlined letters indicate that the syllable should be stressed. In Polish, stress falls on the penultimate syllable: *autobus*, *szkoła*. In some words of foreign origin (mostly Latin and Greek), stress is assigned to the third syllable from the end of the word: *uniwersytet*.

CONSONANTS

Letter	Approximate Pronunciation	Symbol	Example	Pronunciation
c	like ts in fits	ts	całwy	*tsah-wyh*
ć, ci	a soft, very short version of chee in cheese	ch'	cień	*ch'yen'**
cz	like ch in church but harder	ch	czapka	*chahp-kah*
dz	like ds in beds	dz	dzwonek	*dzvoh-nehk*
drz, dż	like j in jam	dj	drzwi	*djvee*
dź, dzi	like ge in genius	dj'	dzień	*dj'yen'*
h,ch	hard, like the ch in Scottish loch	h	chleb	*hlehp*
j	like y in yes	y	jutro	*yoo-troh*
ł	like w in win	w	łóżko	*woozh-koh*
ń, ni	like ni in onion	n'	nie	*n'yeh*
r	rolled, distinct at the end of words	r	rower	*roh-vehr*
sz	like sh in shot but harder	sh	szkoła	*shkoh-wah*

Letter	Approximate Pronunciation	Symbol	Example	Pronunciation
ś, si	soft, very short version of shee in sheep	**sh'**	**śmieci**	_sh'myeh-ch'ee_
w	like v in very	**v**	**woda**	_voh-dah_
ź, zi	like s in pleasure but softer	**zh'**	**źródło**	_zh'rood-woh_
ż, rz	like s in pleasure but harder	**zh**	**żaba**	_zhah-bah_

Letters b, d, f, k, l, m, n, p, s, t, z are pronounced approximately as in English.
* The apostrophe (') in phonetics indicates a softening of the sound.

Like most other European languages, Polish has its origin in Sanskrit and is part of the Indo-European group. It is one of 14 Slavic languages. It is a phonetic language, i.e. there is a good correlation of sound to spelling and the pronunciation is much more systematic than that of English.

VOWELS

Letter	Approximate Pronunciation	Symbol	Example	Pronunciation
a	like a in father	ah	dach	*dahh*
e	like e in ten	eh	bez	*behs*
i	like ee in keen	ee	kino	*kee-noh*
o	like o in so	oh	okno	*ohk-noh*
u, ó	like u in put	oo	sufit	*soo-fit*
y	like i in fit	yh	buty	*boo-tyh*
ą	1. nasal, like an in fiancé, at the end of a word	1. ohm	1. są	1. *sohm*
	2. pronounced ohn before a consonant	2. ohn	2. kąt	2. *kohnt*
	3. pronounced ohm before b and p	3. ohm	3. ząb	3. *zohmb*
ę	1. ehn before a consonant	1. ehn	1. ręka	1. *rehn-kah*
	2. ehm before b and p	2. ehm	2. kępa	2. *kehm-pah*
	3. eh when final in a word	3. eh	3. tę	3. *teh*

HOW TO USE THE APP

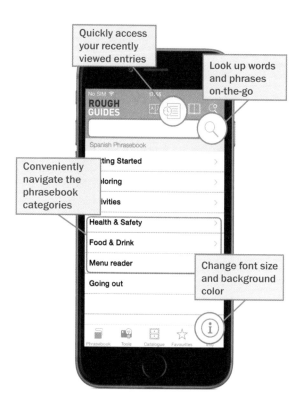

Quickly access your recently viewed entries

Look up words and phrases on-the-go

Conveniently navigate the phrasebook categories

Change font size and background color

Save the most useful everyday words and phrases to your Favorites

Use the Flash Cards Quiz to learn and memorize new words easily

Take all digital advantages of the app: listen to words and phrases pronounced by native speakers

No SIM

Spanish Phrasebook

Can you recommend a good restaurant/ bar?
¿Puede recomend... buen

restaurante/bar?
pweh•deh reh•koh•_mehn_ _dahr_•meh oon bwehn rehs•taw•_rahn_•teh/bahr

Is there a t...

Phrasebook   Tools   Catalogue   Favourites   Info

To learn how to Activate the app, see the inside back cover of this phrasebook.

GRAMMAR

In Polish, there are two forms for you: **ty** (singular) and **wy** (plural). These are used when talking to relatives, close friends and children as well as among young people. When addressing someone in a formal situation use **pan** (Mr/sir), **pani** (Mrs/Ms/ma'am [madam]) or **państwo** (for groups).

REGULAR VERBS

Polish verbs are conjugated based on person, number, tense and gender. Following are the present, past and future forms of the verbs **robić** (to do) and **mieć** (to have).
The following abbreviations are used in this section: sing. = singular; pl. = plural; fml. = formal;

ROBIĆ	FDH	PRESENT	PAST	FUTURE
I	ja	robię	robiłem m robiłam f	*będę robić*
you	ty	robisz	robiłeś m robiłaś f	*będziesz robić*
he/sir	on/pan	robi	robił m	*będzie robić*
she/ madam	ona/pani	robi	robiła f	*będzie robić*
it	ono	robi	robiło	*będzie robić*
we	my	robimy	robiliśmy m robiłyśmy f	*będziemy robić*
you	wy	robicie	robiliście m robiłyście f	*będziecie robić*
they	oni m/ one f	robią	robili m robiły f	*będą robić*
(pl. fml.)	państwo			

MIEĆ	FDH	PRESENT	PAST	FUTURE
I	ja	man	miałem *m* miałam *f*	*będę mieć*
you	ty	masz	miałeś *m* miałaś *f*	*będziesz mieć*
he/sir	on/pan	ma	miał *m*	*będzie mieć*
she/ madam	ona/pani	ma	miała *f*	*będzie mieć*
it	ono	ma	miało	*będzie mieć*
we	my	mamy	mieliśmy *m* mialyśmy *f*	*będziemy mieć*
you	wy	macie	mieliście *m* miałyście *f*	*będziecie mieć*
they	oni *m/* one *f*	mają	mieli *m* miały *f*	*będą mieć*
(pl. fml.)	państwo			

IRREGULAR VERBS

Irregular verbs are not conjugated by following the normal rules. Following are two common irregular verbs, **być** (to be) and **iść** (to go).

MIEĆ	FDH	PRESENT	PAST	FUTURE
I	ja	jestem	byłem *m* byłam *f*	*będę*
you	ty	jesteś	byłeś *m* byłaś *f*	*będziesz*
he/sir	on/pan	jest	był *m*	*będzie*
she/ madam	ona/pani	jest	była *f*	*będzie*
it	ono	jest	było	*będzie*
we	my	jesteśmy	byliśmy *m* byłyśmy *f*	*będziemy*
you	wy	jesteście	byliście *m* byłyście *f*	*będziecie*

they	oni *m*/	są	byli *m*	będą
	one *f*		były *f*	
(pl. fml.)	państwo			

MIEĆ	FDH	PRESENT	PAST	FUTURE
I	ja	idę	szedłem *m*	*będę iść*
			szłam *f*	
you	ty	idziesz	szedłeś *m*	*będziesz iść*
			szłaś *f*	
he/sir	on/pan	idzie	szedł *m*	*będzie iść*
she/	ona/pani	idzie	szła *f*	*będzie iść*
madam				
it	ono	idzie	szło	*będzie iść*
we	my	idziemy	szliśmy *m*	*będziemy iść*
			szłyśmy *f*	
you	wy	idziecie	szliście *m*	*będziecie iść*
			szłyście *f*	
they	oni *m*/	idą	szli *m*	*będą iść*
	one *f*		szły *f*	
(pl. fml.)	państwo			

NOUNS

Nouns in Polish are either masculine, feminine or neuter. Masculine nouns usually end in a consonant. Feminine nouns usually end in –a or, less often, –i. Neuter nouns end in –ę or –o. Most masculine and feminine nouns, when plural, end in –y or in –i; most neuter nouns in –a.

The endings of nouns vary according to their role in the sentence. There are seven different cases (roles) in both the singular and plural.

There are no articles (a, an, the) in Polish.

WORD ORDER

Word order in Polish is usually as in English, i.e., subject-verb-object. However, word order can be more flexible, because the word endings indicate the role of each word in the sentence.

Example: **Ania dała książkę Markowi. = Ania dała Markowi książkę. = Ania Markowi dała książkę.** (Ania gave Marek a book.)

To ask a question in Polish:

1. use **czy**

Example: **Czy to pan Kowalski?** Is it Mr. Kowalski?

2. add rising intonation to an affirmative statement

Example: **Pan Kowalski?** Mr. Kowalski?

3. use question words

gdzie, kiedy, kto, co where, when, who, what

Example: **Gdzie jesteś?** Where are you?

Kiedy wrócisz? When are you coming back?

Co będziemy robić? What are we going to do?

NEGATIONS

To form a negative sentence, add **nie** (not) before the verb. Note that noun endings may change.

Example: **Mam bilet.** I have a ticket.

Nie mam biletu. I don't have a ticket.

IMPERATIVES

Imperative sentences are formed by adding the appropriate ending to the verb stem.
Example: Go!

you	ty	Idź!
he/sir	on/pan	Niech idzie!
she/madam	ona/pani	Niech idzie!
it	ono	Niech idzie!
we	my	Idźmy!
you	wy	Idźcie!
they (pl. fml.)	oni *m*/one *f*	Niech idą!
		Niech państwo idą!

ADJECTIVES

Adjectives must agree in gender, number and case with the nouns they modify. Masculine adjectives usually end in −y or −i. The feminine and neuter endings are −a and −e, respectively.

Examples: **To duży m dom m.** This is a big house.
             To duża f szkoła f. This is a big school.
             To duże dziecko. This is a big child.

COMPARATIVES & SUPERLATIVES

The comparative is usually formed by adding **–szy** *m*/**–sza** *f*/**–sze** *(neuter)* and the superlative by adding **naj…–szy** *m*/**–sza** *f*/**–sze** *(neuter)*.

Example:

tani (cheap)	**tańszy**	**najtańszy**

Less common adjectives often use the complex comparative and superlative form:

comparative = **bardziej** (more) + adjective
superlative = **najbardziej** (the most) + adjective

Example:

tradycyjny (traditional)	**bardziej tradycyjny**	**najbardziej tradycyjny**

ADVERBS

Some adverbs in Polish are formed from adjectives by adding the ending **–o**, but there is no fixed rule.

Examples: **To szybki samochód.** This is a fast car. (adjective)
Robert jeździ szybko samochodem. Robert drives his car fast. (adverb)

PRACTICALITIES

THE BASICS

NUMBERS

NEED TO KNOW

0	**zero**	*zeh • roh*
1	**jeden**	*yeh • dehn*
2	**dwa**	*dvah*
3	**trzy**	*tshyh*
4	**cztery**	*chteh • ryh*
5	**pięć**	*pyehn'ch'*
6	**sześć**	*shehsh'ch'*
7	**siedem**	*sh'yeh • dehm*
8	**osiem**	*oh • sh'yehm*
9	**dziewięć**	*dj'yeh • vyehn'ch'*
10	**dziesięć**	*dj'yeh • sh'yehn'ch'*
11	**jedenaście**	*yeh • deh • nahsh' • ch'yeh*
12	**dwanaście**	*dvah • nahsh' • ch'yeh*

13	**trzynaście**	*tshyh • nahsh´ • ch'yeh*
14	**czternaście**	*chtehr • nahsh´ • ch'yeh*
15	**piętnaście**	*pyeht • nahsh´ • ch'yeh*
16	**szesnaście**	*shehs • nahsh´ • ch'yeh*
17	**siedemnaście**	*sh'yehdehm • nahsh´ • ch'yeh*
18	**osiemnaście**	*oh • sh'yehm • nahsh´ • ch'yeh*
19	**dziewiętnaście**	*dj'yeh • vyeht • nahsh´ • ch'yeh*
20	**dwadzieścia**	*dvah • dj'yehsh´ • ch'yah*
21	**dwadzieścia jeden**	*dvah • dj'yehsh´ • ch'yah yeh • dehn*
22	**dwadzieścia dwa**	*dvah • dj'yehsh´ • ch'yah dvah*
30	**trzydzieści**	*tshyh • dj'yehsh´ • ch'ee*
40	**czterdzieści**	*chtehr • dj'yehsh´ • ch'ee*
50	**pięćdziesiąt**	*pyehn´ • dj'yeh • sh'yohnt*
60	**sześćdziesiąt**	*shehsh´ • dj'yeh • sh'yont*
70	**siedemdziesiąt**	*sh'yeh • dehm • dj'yeh • sh'yohnt*
80	**osiemdziesiąt**	*oh • sh'yehm • dj'yeh • sh'yohnt*

90	**dziewięćdziesiąt**
	dj'eh • vyen' • dj'yeh • sh'ohnt
100	**sto**
	stoh
101	**sto jeden**
	stoh • yeh • dehn
200	**dwieście**
	dvyehsh' • ch'yeh
500	**pięćset**
	pyehnch' • seht
1,000	**tysiąc**
	tyh • sh'yohnts
10,000	**dziesięć tysięcy**
	dj'yeh • sh'yehn'ch' tyh • sh'yen • tsyh
1,000,000	**milion**
	meel • yohn

ORDINAL NUMBERS

first	**pierwszy**
	pyehr • vshyh
second	**drugi**
	droo • gee
third	**trzeci**
	tsheh • ch'ee
fourth	**czwarty**
	chfahr • tyh
fifth	**piąty**
	pyohn • tyh
once	**raz**
	rahs

twice	**dwa razy**
	dvah <u>rah</u> • zyh
three times	**trzy razy**
	tshyh <u>rah</u> • zyh

In Polish, as in the majority of European countries, a comma is used in place of a decimal point, and gaps are used in long numbers in place of commas. Example: 1 234 567,89 **jeden milion, dwieście trzydzieści cztery tysiące, pięćset sześćdziesiąt siedem, osiemdziesiąt dziewięć**.

TIME

NEED TO KNOW

What time is it?	**Czy może mi pan powiedzieć, która godzina?**
	chyh moh • zheh mee pahn poh • vyeh • dj'yehch' ktoo • rah goh • dj'ee • nah
five after [past] five	**pięć po piątej**
	pyehn'ch' poh pyohn • tehy
quarter to nine	**za piętnaście dziewiąta**
	zah pyeht • nahsh' • ch'yeh dj'yeh • vyohn • tah
ten to seven	**za dziesięć siódma**
	zah dj'yeh • sh'yehn'ch' sh'yood • mah
5:30 a.m./p.m.	**piąta trzydzieści rano/siedemnasta trzydzieści**
	pyohn • tah tshyh • dj'yehsh' • ch'ee rah • noh/sh'yeh • dehm • nahs • tah tshyh • dj'yehsh' • ch'ee
It's noon [midday].	**Jest południe.**
	yehst poh • wood • n'yeh
It's midnight.	**Jest północ.**
	yehst poow • nohts

In Poland, time is expressed using the 24-hour clock. However, in ordinary conversation, time is usually expressed using numbers 1 to 12 with the addition of **rano** (morning), **po południu** (afternoon) or **wieczorem** (evening).

DAYS

NEED TO KNOW

Monday	**poniedziałek**	
	poh • n'yeh • dj'yah' • wehk	
Tuesday	**wtorek**	
	ftoh • rehk	
Wednesday	**środa**	
	sh'roh • dah	
Thursday	**czwartek**	
	chfahr • tehk	
Friday	**piątek**	
	pyohn • tehk	
Saturday	**sobota**	
	soh • boh • tah	
Sunday	**niedziela**	
	n'yeh • dj'yeh • lah	

DATES

yesterday	**wczoraj**	
	fchoh • rahy	
today	**dzisiaj**	
	dj'ee • sh'yahy	
tomorrow	**jutro**	
	yoot • roh	
day	**dzień**	
	dj'yehn'	
week	**tydzień**	
	tyh • dj'yehn'	

month	**miesiąc**
	myeh • sh'ohnts
year	**rok**
	rohk

MONTHS

January	**styczeń**
	styh • chehn'
February	**luty**
	loo • tyh
March	**marzec**
	mah • zhehts
April	**kwiecień**
	kfyeh • ch'yehn'
May	**maj**
	mahy
June	**czerwiec**
	chehr • vyehts
July	**lipiec**
	lee • pyehts
August	**sierpień**
	sh'yehr • pyehn'

September	**wrzesień**
	vzheh • sh'yehn'
October	**październik**
	pahzh' • dj'yehr • n'eek
November	**listopad**
	lees • toh • paht
December	**grudzień**
	groo • dj'yehn'

SEASONS

spring	**wiosna**
	vyohs • nah
summer	**lato**
	lah • toh
fall [autumn]	**jesień**
	yeh • sh'yehn'
winter	**zima**
	zh'ee • mah

HOLIDAYS

January 1: New Year's Day, **Nowy Rok**
January 6: Epiphany, **Trzech Króli**
March/April: Easter (moveable), **Wielkanoc**
May 1: Labor Day, **Święto 1 Maja**
May 3: Constitution Day, **Konstytucja 3 Maja**
Thursday in May/June: Corpus Christi (moveable), **Boże Ciało**
August 15: Assumption Day, **Wniebowzięcie**
November 1: All Saints' Day, **Wszystkich Świętych**
November 11: Independence Day, **Święto Niepodległości**
December 25 & 26: Christmas, **Boże Narodzenie**

ARRIVAL & DEPARTURE

NEED TO KNOW

I'm here on vacation/business.	**Przyjechałem** *m*/**Przyjechałam** *f* **tutaj na wakacje/łużbowo.** *pshyh • yeh • hah • wehm/ pshyh • yeh • hah • wahm too • tahy nah vah • kahts • yeh/swoozh • boh • voh*
I'm going to…	**Jadę do…** *yah • deh doh…*
I'm staying at the… Hotel.	**Zatrzymałem** *m*/**Zatrzymałam** *f* **się w Hotelu…** *zah • tshyh • mah • wehm/ zah • tshyh • mah • wahm sh'yeh fhoh • teh • loo…*

YOU MAY HEAR...

Bilet/Paszport, proszę.
bee • leht/pahsh • pohrt proh • sheh
please.

Your ticket/
passport,

Jaki jest cel pana wizyty?
yah • kee yehst tsehl pah • nah
vee • zyh • tyh

What's the
purpose of your
visit?

Gdzie pan się zatrzymał?
gdj'yeh pahn sh'yeh zah • tshyh • mahw

Where are you
staying?

Jak długo pan tu będzie?
yahk dwoo • goh pahn too behn • dj'ye

How long are you
staying?

Z kim pan tutaj jest?
skeem pahn too • tahy yehst

Who are you here
with?

When addressing a man in a formal situation, use
pan (sir); when addressing a woman, use **pani** (ma'am or
madam). Throughout this phrase book **pan** is used for the
sake of simplicity. When speaking to a woman, be sure to
substitute **pani** for **pan**.

BORDER CONTROL

I'm just passing
through.

Jestem tu tylko przejazdem.
yeh • stehm too tyhl • koh
psheh • yahz • dehm

I would like to
declare...

Chciałbym m/**Chciałabym** f
zadeklarować...
hch'yahw • byhm/hch'yah • wah • byhm
zah • dehk • lah • roh • vahch'...

I have nothing to declare.

Nie mam nic do oclenia.
n'yeh mahm n'eets doh ohts • leh • n'yah

YOU MAY HEAR...

Czy ma pan coś do oclenia?
chyh mah pahn tsohsh' doh ohts • leh • n'yah

Anything to declare?

Musi pan zapłacić za to cło.
moo • sh'ee pahn zah • pwa • ch'eech' zah toh tswoh

You must pay duty on this.

Proszę otworzyć torbę/walizkę. your
proh • sheh oht • foh • zhyhch' tohr • beh/ vah • lees • keh

Please open bag/suitcase.

YOU MAY SEE...

ODPRAWA CELNA	customs
TOWARY BEZCŁOWE	duty-free goods
TOWARY DO OCLENIA	goods to declare
NIC DO OCLENIA	nothing to declare
KONTROLA PASZPORTOWA	passport control
POLICJA	police
DLA PERSONELU	staff only

MONEY

NEED TO KNOW

Where's…?	**Gdzie jest…?**
	gdj'yeh yehst…
the ATM	**bankomat**
	bahn • koh • maht
the bank	**bank**
	bahnk
the currency exchange office	**kantor**
	kahn • tohr
When does the bank open/close?	**O której otwierają/zamykają bank?**
	oh ktoo • rehy oht • fyeh • rah • yohm/ zah • myh • kah • yohm bahnk
I'd like to change dollars/pounds into zlotys.	**Chciałbym** *m*/**Chciałabym** *f* **wymienić dolary/funty na złotówki.**
	hch'yahw • byhm/hch'yah • wah • byhm vyh • myeh • n'eech' do • lah • ryh/ foon • tyh nah zwoh • toof • kee
I want to cash some travelers checks.	**Chcę zrealizować czeki podróżne.**
	htseh zreh • ah • lee • zoh • vahch' cheh • kee pohd • roozh • neh

AT THE BANK

I'd like to change money.	**Chciałbym** *m*/**Chciałabym** *f* **wymienić pieniądze.**
	hch'yahw • byhm/hch'yah • wah • byhm vyh • myeh • n'eech' pyeh • n'yohn • dzeh
What's the exchange rate?	**Jaki jest kurs wymiany?**
	yah • kee yehst koors vyh • myah • nyh

How much is the fee?	**Jaka jest prowizja?**
	yah • kah yest proh • veez • yah
I've lost my travelers checks/ credit cards.	**Zgubiłem** *m*/**Zgubiłam** *f* **czeki podróżne/ karty kredytowe.**
	zgoo • bee • wehm/zgoo • bee • wahm cheh • kee pohd • roozh • neh/kahr • tyh kreh • dyh • toh • veh
My card was stolen.	**Ukradli mi kartę.**
	oo • krahd • lee mee kahr • teh
My card doesn't work.	**Moja karta nie działa.**
	moh • yah kahr • tah n'yeh dj'yah • wah

For Numbers, see page 20.

YOU MAY SEE...

The currency in Poland is the **złoty**; one **złoty** is made up of 100 **groszy**. Soon Poland may adopt the euro as its national currency; until then **złoty** is the accepted form of payment.
Coins: 1, 2, 5, 10, 20, 50 **groszy**; 1, 2, 5 **złoty**.
Bills: 10, 20, 50, 100, 200 **złoty**.

Prices in Poland generally include **VAT** (sales tax). The price you will pay is the price displayed on the sales tag.

Banks usually open between 8:00 a.m. and 6:00 p.m. When changing cash and travelers checks, you will need to show your passport. Numerous **kantory** (currency exchange offices) provide exchange services and usually have a better exchange rate than banks. Some large hotels will exchange cash and travelers checks for their guests. In cities and larger towns you'll find **bankomaty**, ATMs that accept various international bank and credit cards. Travelers checks are not currently accepted in stores and hotels.

YOU MAY SEE...

WŁÓŻ KARTĘ	insert credit card
WYBIERZ JĘZYK	select language
WPROWADŹ PIN	enter your PIN
WCIŚNIJ KLAWISZ	press key
WYPŁATA GOTÓWKI	cash withdrawal
INNA KWOTA	different amount
STAN RACHUNKU	balance inquiry
WOLNE ŚRODKI	available balance
AKCEPTUJ	enter
ANULUJ	cancel
POPRAW	clear
KONTYNUUJ	next
KONIEC	end
POTWIERDZENIE	receipt

CONVERSATION

NEED TO KNOW

Hello	**Dzień dobry.**
	dj'yehn' <u>dohb</u> • ryh
How are you?	**Jak się pan ma?**
	yahk sh'yeh pahn mah
Fine, thanks.	**W porządku, dziękuję.**
	fpoh • <u>zhohnt</u> • koo dz'yehn • koo • yeh
Excuse me!	**Przepraszam!**
	psheh • <u>prah</u> • shahm
Do you speak English?	**Mówi pan po angielsku?**
	<u>moo</u> • vee pahn poh ahn • <u>gyehl</u> • skoo
What's your name?	**Jak się pan nazywa?**
	yahk sh'yeh pahn nah • <u>zyh</u> • vah
My name is…	**Nazywam się…**
	nah • <u>zyh</u> • vahm sh'yeh…
Pleased to meet you.	**Miło mi pana poznać.**
	<u>mee</u> • woh mee <u>pah</u> • nah <u>pohz</u> • nahch'
Where are you from?	**Skąd pan jest?**
	skohnt pahn yehst
I'm from the U.S./U.K.	**Jestem z USA/Wielkiej Brytanii.**
	<u>yehs</u> • tehm z oo • ehs • <u>ah/vyehl</u> • kyehy bryh • <u>tah</u> • n'ee
What do you do for a living?	**Czym się pan zajmuje?**
	chyhm sh'yeh pahn zahy • <u>moo</u> • yeh
I work for…	**Pracuję w…**
	prah • <u>tsoo</u> • yeh v…
I'm a student.	**Studiuję.**
	stoo • <u>dyoo</u> • yeh

I'm retired.	**Jestem na emeryturze.**
	yehs • tehm nah
	eh • meh • ryh • too • zheh
Do you like…?	**Lubi pan…?**
	loo • bee pahn…
Goodbye.	**Do widzenia.**
	doh vee • dzeh • n'yah
See you later.	**Do zobaczenia.**
	doh zoh • bah • cheh • n'yah

LANGUAGE DIFFICULTIES

Do you speak English?	**Mówi pan po angielsku?**
	moo • vee pahn po ahn • gyehls • koo
Does anyone here speak English?	**Czy ktoś tu zna angielski?**
	chyh ktohsh' too znah ahn • gyehls • kee
I don't speak much Polish.	**Słabo mówię po polsku.**
	swah • boh moo • vyeh poh pohls • koo
Can you speak more slowly?	**Proszę mówić wolniej.**
	proh • sheh moo • veech' vohl • n'yehy
Can you repeat that?	**Proszę powtórzyć.**
	proh • sheh pohf • too • zhyhch'

Excuse me? [Pardon?]	**Słucham?**
	swoo • hahm
What was that?	**Co pan powiedział?**
	tsoh pahn poh • vyeh • dj'yahw
Can you spell it?	**Może pan to przeliterować?**
	moh • zheh pahn toh
	psheh • leeh • teh • roh • vahch'
Can you write it down?	**Może pan mi to napisać?**
	moh • zheh pahn mee toh
	nah • pee • sahch'
Can you translate this into English for me?	**Może pan mi to przetłumaczyć na angielski?**
	moh • zheh pahn mee toh
	psheh • twoo • mah • chyhch' nah
	ahn • gyehl • skyh
What does this mean?	**Co to znaczy?**
	tsoh toh znah • chyh
I understand.	**Rozumiem.**
	roh • zoo • myehm
I don't understand.	**Nie rozumiem.**
	n'yeh roh • zoo • myehm
Do you understand?	**Rozumie pan?**
	roh • zoo • myeh pahn

YOU MAY HEAR…

Słabo mówię po angielsku.
swah • boh moo • vyeh poh
ahn • gyehls • koo

I speak only a little English.

Nie mówię po angielsku.
n'yeh moo • vyeh poh ahn • gyehls • koo

I don't speak English.

In olden times, it was customary for men to kiss women's hands as a sign of respect upon greeting. Today men and women simply say hello or kiss each other on the cheek if they are good friends. In most situations you can say **dzień dobry**, good morning or hello. With relatives, friends and children you can simply say **cześć**, meaning 'hi'.

MAKING FRIENDS

Hello./Hi!	**Dzień dobry./Cześć!**
	dj'yehn' dohb • ryh/chehsh'ch'
Good morning.	**Dzień dobry.**
	dj'yehn' dohb • ryh
Good evening.	**Dobry wieczór.**
	dohb • ryh vyeh • choor
My name is…	**Nazywam się…**
	nah • zyh • vahm sh'yeh…
What's your name?	**Jak się pan nazywa?**
	yahk sh'yeh pahn nah • zyh • vah
I'd like to introduce you to…	**Chciałbym** m **/Chciałabym** f **pana przedstawić…**
	hch'yahw • byhm/hch'yah • wah • byhm pah • nah psheht • stah • veech'…
Pleased to meet you.	**Miło mi pana poznać.**
	mee • woh mee pah • nah pohz • nahch'
How are you?	**Jak się pan ma?**
	yahk sh'yeh pahn mah
Fine, thanks.	**W porządku, dziękuję.**
	fpoh • zhohnt • koo dz'yehn • koo • yeh
And you?	**A pan?**
	ah pahn

TRAVEL TALK

I'm here…	**Jestem tutaj.**	
	yehs • tehm too • tay	
on business	**służbowo**	
	swoozh • boh • voh	
on vacation	**na wakacjach**	
	nah vah • kahts • yahh	
I'm studying.	**Studiuję.**	
	stood • yoo • yeh	
I'm staying for…	**Będę tu…**	
	beh • deh too…	
I've been here…	**Jestem tu…**	
	yehs • tehm too…	
a day	**jeden dzień**	
	yeh • dehn dj'yehn'	
a week	**tydzień**	
	tyh • dj'yehn'	
a month	**miesiąc**	
	myeh • sh'yohnts	
Where are you from?	**Skąd pan jest?**	
	skohnt pahn yehst	
I'm from…	**Jestem z…**	
	yehs • tehm z…	

For Numbers, see page 20.

PERSONAL

Who are you with?	**Z kim pan tu jest?**	
	skeem pahn too yehst	
I'm here alone.	**Jestem sam** *m/***sama** *f*	
	yehs • tehm sahm/sah • mah	
I'm with…	**Jestem z…**	
	yehs • tehm z…	

my husband/wife	**moim mężem/moją żoną**
	moh • eem mehn • zhehm/moh • yohm zhoh • nohm
my boyfriend/ girlfriend	**moim chłopakiem/moją dziewczyną**
	moh • eem hwoh • pah • kyehm/moh • yohm dj'yehf • chyh • nohm
a friend	**przyjacielem** *m*/**przyjaciółką** *f*
	pshyh • yah • ch'yeh • lehm/ pshyh • yah • ch'yoow • kohm
friends	**przyjaciółmi**
	pshyh • yah • ch'yoow • myh
a colleague	**kolegą** *m*/**koleżanką** *f* **z pracy**
	koh • leh • gohm/koh • leh • zhahn • kohm sprah • tsyh
colleagues	**kolegami** *m*/**koleżankami** *f* **z pracy**
	koh • leh • gah • myh/ koh • leh • zhahn • kah • myh sprah • tsyh
When's your birthday?	**Kiedy ma pan urodziny?**
	k'yeh • dyh mah pahn oo • roh • dj'ee • nyh
How old are you?	**Ile ma pan lat?**
	ee • leh mah pahn laht
I'm…	**Mam…lat.**
	mahm…laht
Are you married?	**Czy jest pan żonaty** *m*/**pani mężatką** *f* **?**
	chyh yehst pahn zhoh • nah • tyh/pah • n'ee mehn • zhaht • kohm
I'm…	**Jestem…**
	yehs • tehm…
single/ in a relationship	**wolny** *m*/**wolna** *f*
	w związku vohl • nyh/vohl • nah/ vzvyohn • skoo
engaged	**zaręczony** *m*/**zaręczona** *f*
	zah • rehn • choh • nyh/ zah • rehn • choh • nah

married	**żonaty** m/**mężatką** f
	zhoh • nah • tyh/ mehn • zhaht • kohm
divorced	**rozwiedziony** m/**rozwiedziona** f
	rohz • vyeh • dj'yoh • nyh/
	rohz • vyeh • dj'yoh • nah
separated	**w separacji**
	fseh • pah • rah • tsee
widowed	**wdowcem** m/**wdową** f
	vdoh • vtsehm/vdoh • vohm
Do you have children/ grandchildren?	**Ma pan dzieci/wnuki?**
	mah pahn dj'yeh • ch'ee/ vnoo • kee

For Numbers, see page 20.

WORK & SCHOOL

What do you do for a living?	**Czym się pan zajmuje?**
	chyhm sh'yeh pahn zahy • moo • yeh?
What are you studying?	**Co pan studiuje?**
	tsoh pahn stood • yoo • yeh
I'm studying…	**Studiuję…**
	stood • yoo • yeh…
I work full time/ part time.	**Pracuję na pełny etat/część etatu.**
	prah • tsoo • yeh nah pehw • nyh eh • taht/ chehn'sh'ch' eh • tah • too
I'm unemployed.	**Nie pracuję.**
	n'yeh prah • tsoo • yeh
I work at home.	**Pracuję w domu.**
	prah • tsoo • yeh vdoh • moo
Who do you work for?	**Gdzie pan pracuje?**
	gdj'yeh pahn prah • tsoo • yeh
I work for…	**Pracuję w…**
	prah • tsoo • yeh v…

Here's my business card. **Oto moja wizytówka.**
_oh_ • toh _moh_ • yah vee • zyh • _toof_ • kah

For Communications, see page 83.

WEATHER

What's the weather forecast? **Jaka jest prognoza pogody?**
yah • kah yehst prohg • _noh_ • zah
poh • _goh_ • dyh

What beautiful/ terrible weather! **Jaka piękna/okropna pogoda!**
yah • kah _pyehnk_ • nah/oh • _krohp_ • nah
poh • _goh_ • dah

It's cool/warm. **Jest chłodno/ciepło.**
yehst _hwohd_ • noh/_ch'yehp_ • wo

It's hot/cold. **Jest gorąco/zimno.**
yehst goh • _rohn_ • tsoh/_zh'eem_ • noh

It's sunny. **Świeci słońce.**
sh'vyeh • ch'ee _swohn'_ • tseh

It's rainy/snowy. **Pada deszcz/śnieg.**
pah • dah dehshch/sh'n'yehk

It's icy. **Jest ślisko.**
yehst _sh'lees_ • koh

Do I need a jacket/ an umbrella? **Mam wziąć kurtkę/parasol?**
mahm vzyohn'ch' _koort_ • keh/
pah • _rah_ • sohl

For Seasons, see page 27.

ON THE WAY

GETTING AROUND

NEED TO KNOW

How do I get to town?	**Jak stąd dojechać do miasta?**
	yahk stohnt doh • <u>yeh</u> • hahch' doh <u>myahs</u> • tah
Where's...?	**Gdzie jest...?**
the airport	*gdj'yeh yehst... lotnisko loht • <u>n'ees</u> • koh*
the train [railway] station	**dworzec kolejowy**
	<u>dvoh</u> • zhehts koh • leh • <u>yoh</u> • vyh
the bus station	**dworzec autobusowy**
	<u>dvoh</u> • zhehts ahw • toh • boo • <u>soh</u> • vyh
the metro [underground] station	**stacja metra**
	<u>stahts</u> • yah <u>meht</u> • rah
Is it far from here?	**Czy to daleko stąd?**
	chyh toh dah • <u>leh</u> • koh stohnt
Where can I buy tickets?	**Gdzie mogę kupić bilety?**
	gdj'yeh <u>moh</u> • geh koo • <u>peech'</u> bee • <u>leh</u> • tyh

A one-way [single]/ round-trip [return] ticket to…
Bilet w jedną stonę/powrotny do…
bee • leht vyehd • nohm stroh • neh/ pohv • roht • nyh doh…

Are there any discounts?
Czy są jakieś zniżki?
chyh sohm yah • kyehsh' zn'eesh • kee

Where can I get a taxi?
Gdzie mogę złapać taksówkę?
gdj'yeh moh • geh zwah • pahch' tahk • soof • keh

Please take me to this address.
Proszę mnie zawieźć pod ten adres.
proh • sheh mn'yeh zah • vyehsh'ch' poht tehn ahd • rehs

Where can I rent a car?
Gdzie mogę wynająć samochód?
gdj'yeh moh • geh vyh • nah • yohn'ch' sah • moh • hoot

Can I have a map, please?
Poproszę mapę.
poh • proh • sheh mah • peh

TICKETS

When's…to Cracow?
O której jest…do Krakowa?
oh ktoo • rehy yehst… doh krah • koh • vah

the (first) bus
(pierwszy) autobus
(pyehr • shyh) ahw • toh • boos

the (next) flight
(następny) samolot
(nahs • tehm • pnyh) sah • moh • loht

the (last) train
(ostatni) pociąg
(ohs • taht • n'ee) poh • ch'yonk

Where can I buy a ticket?
Gdzie mogę kupić bilet?
gdj'yeh moh • geh koo • peech' bee • leht

One/two ticket(s), please.
Jeden bilet/Dwa bilety proszę.
yeh • dehn bee • leht/dvah bee • leh • tyh proh • sheh

A...ticket.	**Bilet...**
	bee • leht...
one-way [single]	**w jedną stronę**
	vyehd • nohm _stroh_ • neh
round-trip [return]	**powrotny**
	pohv • _roht_ • nyh
first class	**w pierwszej klasie**
	fpyehr • shehy _klah_ • sh'yeh
economy class	**w klasie turystycznej**
	fklah • sh'yeh too • ryhs • _tyhch_ • nehy
How much?	**Ile to kosztuje?**
	_ee_ • leh toh kohsh • _too_ • yeh
Is there a discount for...?	**Czy jest zniżka dla...?**
	chyh yehst _zn'eesh_ • kah dlah...
children	**dzieci**
	_dj'ye_ • ch'ee
students	**studentów**
	stoo • _dehn_ • toof
senior citizens	**emerytów**
	eh • meh • _ryh_ • toof
I have an e-ticket.	**Mam bilet elektroniczny.**
	mahm _bee_ • leht eh • lehk • troh • _n'eech_ • nyh
Can I buy a ticket on the bus/train?	**Czy można kupić bilet w autobusie/ pociągu?**
	chyh _mohzh_ • nah _koo_ • peech' bee • leht v ahw • toh • _boo_ • sh'yeh/poh • _ch'yohn_ • goo
I'd like to...my reservation.	**Chciałbym** m/**Chciałabym** f...**moją rezerwację.**
	hch'yahw • byhm/hch'yah • wah • byhm... _moh_ • yohm reh • zehr • _vahts_ • yeh
cancel	**odwołać**
	ohd • _voh_ • wahch'
change	**zmienić**
	zmyeh • n'eech'

| confirm | **potwierdzić** |
| | *poh • tfyehr • dj'eech'* |

For Money, see page 31.

AIRPORT TRANSFER

How much is a taxi to the airport?	**Ile kosztuje taksówka na lotnisko?**
	ee • leh kohsh • too • yeh tahk • soof • kah nah loht • n'ees • koh
To…Airport, please.	**Na lotnisko…proszę.**
	nah loht • n'ees • koh…proh • sheh
My airline is…	**Lecę liniami…**
	leh • tseh lee • n'yah • mee…
My flight leaves at…	**Mam samolot o…**
	mahm sah • moh • loht oh…
I'm in a hurry.	**Spieszę się.**
	spyeh • sheh sh'yeh
Can you drive faster/ slower?	**Mógłby pan jechać szybciej/wolniej?**
	moogw • byh pahn yeh • hahch' shyhp • ch'yehy/vohl • n'yehy

For Time, see page 24.

YOU MAY SEE…

PRZYLOTY	arrivals
ODLOTY	departures
ODBIÓR BAGAŻU	baggage claim
ODLOTY KRAJOWE	domestic flights
ODLOTY MIĘDZYNARODOWE	international flights
STANOWISKO ODPRAWY	check-in
WYJŚCIA	departure gates
NIC DO OCLENIA	nothing to declare
TOWARY DO OCLENIA	goods to declare
INFORMACJA CELNA	customs information
WOLNY OBSZAR CELNY	duty-free zone

YOU MAY HEAR…

Jakimi liniami pan leci?
yah • <u>kee</u> • mee lee • <u>n'yah</u> • mee pahn <u>leh</u> • ch'ee

What airline are you flying?

Lot krajowy czy zagraniczny?
loht krah • <u>yoh</u> • wyh chyh zah • grah • <u>n'eech</u> • nyh

Domestic or international flight?

Który terminal?
<u>ktoo</u> • ryh tehr • <u>mee</u> • nahl

What terminal?

CHECKING IN

Where's check-in?	**Gdzie jest stanowisko odprawy?**
	gdj'yeh yehst stah • noh • <u>vees</u> • koh
	oht • <u>prah</u> • vyh
My name is…	**Nazywam się…**
	nah • <u>zyh</u> • vahm sh'yeh…
I'm going to…	**Lecę do…**
	<u>leh</u> • tseh doh…
How much luggage is	**Ile bagażu mogę wziąć?**
allowed?	<u>ee</u> • leh bah • <u>gah</u> • zhoo <u>moh</u> • geh
	wzh'yohn'ch'
Which terminal does	**Z którego terminalu odlatuje lot**
flight…leave from?	**numer…?**
	sktoo • <u>reh</u> • goh tehr mee • <u>nah</u> • loo
	ohd • lah • <u>too</u> • yeh loht <u>noo</u> • mehr…
Which gate does	**Które wyjście jest dla lotu numer…?**
flight…leave from?	<u>ktoo</u> • reh vyhy • sh'ch'yeh yehst dlah
	<u>loh</u> • too <u>noo</u> • mehr…
I'd like a window/	**Chciałbym** m/**Chciałabym** f **miejsce przy**
an aisle seat.	**oknie/ przejściu.**
	<u>hch'yahw</u> • byhm/<u>hch'yah</u> • wah • byhm
	<u>myehys</u> • tseh pshyh <u>ohk</u> • n'yeh/
	pshehy • sh'ch'yoo

Can I take this on board?	**Czy mogę to wziąć jako bagaż podręczny?** chyh <u>moh</u> • geh toh vzh'yohn'ch' <u>yah</u> • koh <u>bah</u> • gahsh pohd • <u>rehn</u> • chnyh
When do we leave/ arrive?	**O której startujemy/lądujemy?** oh <u>ktoo</u> • rehy <u>stahr</u> • too • yeh • myh/ lohn • doo • <u>yeh</u> • myh

---

YOU MAY HEAR...

Proszę następną osobę! <u>proh</u> • sheh nah • <u>stehmp</u> • nohm oh • <u>soh</u> • beh	Next person, please!
Poproszę paszport/bilet. poh • <u>proh</u> • sheh <u>pahsh</u> • pohrt/<u>bee</u> • leht	Your passport/ ticket, please.
Ma pan jakiś bagaż do nadania? mah pahn <u>yah</u> • keesh' <u>bah</u> • gahsh doh nah • <u>dah</u> • n'yah	Are you checking in any luggage?
Ma pan nadbagaż. mah pahn nahd • <u>bah</u> • gash	You have excess luggage.
Czy pan się sam pakował? chyh pahn sh'yeh sahm pah • <u>koh</u> • vahw	Did you pack these bags yourself?
Proszę opróżnić kieszenie. <u>proh</u> • sheh ohp • <u>roozh</u> • n'eech' kyeh • <u>sheh</u> • n'yeh	Please empty your pockets.
Proszę zdjąć buty. <u>proh</u> • sheh zdyohn'ch' <u>boo</u> • tyh	Please take off your shoes.
Zapraszamy pasażerów na pokład samolotu do..., rejs numer... zah • prah • <u>shah</u> • myh pah • sah • <u>zheh</u> • roov nah <u>pohk</u> • wahd sah • moh • <u>loh</u> • too doh...rehys <u>noo</u> • mehr...	Now boarding flight number... to...

Is flight…delayed?	**Czy lot…jest opóźniony?**
	chyh loht…yehst oh • poozh´ • n'yoh • nyh
How late will it be?	**O ile jest opóźniony?**
	oh ee • leh yehst oh • poozh´ • n'yoh • nyh

LUGGAGE

Where is/are…?	**Gdzie jest/są…?**
	gdj'yeh yehst/sohm…
the luggage carts [trolleys]	**wózki bagażowe**
	voos • kee bah • gah • zhoh • veh
luggage lockers/ baggage room	**skrytki bagażowe/przechowalnia bagażu**
	skryht • kee bah • gah • zhoh • veh/ psheh • hoh • vahl • n'yah bah • gah • zhoo
the baggage claim	**odbiór bagażu**
	ohd • byoor bah • gah • zhoo
My luggage has been lost.	**Zgubili mój bagaż.**
	zgoo • bee • lee mooy bah • gahsh
My baggage has been stolen.	**Ukradli mi bagaż.**
	oo • krahd • lee mee bah • gahsh
My suitcase was damaged.	**Moja walizka została uszkodzona.**
	moh • yah vah • lees • kah zohs • tah • wah oosh • koh • dzoh • nah

FINDING YOUR WAY

Where is/are…?	**Gdzie jest/są…?**
	gdj'yeh yehst/sohm…
the currency exchange office	**kantor**
	kahn • tohr
the exit	**wyjście**
	vyhsh'ch'yeh
the taxis	**taksówki**
	tahk • soof • kee

Where is the car rental [hire]?	**Gdzie można wynająć samochód?**
	gdj'yeh mohzh • nah wyh • nah • yohn'ch' sah • moh • hoot
Is there…into town?	**Czy można stąd dojechać…do centrum?**
	chyh mohzh • nah stohnt doh • yeh • hahch'…doh tsehn • troom
a bus	**autobusem**
	ahw • toh • boo • sehm
a train	**pociągiem**
	poh • ch'yohn • gyehm
a metro	**metrem**
	meht • rehm

For Asking Directions, see page 64.

TRAIN

Where's the train station?	**Gdzie jest dworzec kolejowy?**
	gdj'yeh yehst dvoh • zhehts koh • leh • yoh • vyh
Is it far from here?	**Czy to daleko stąd?**
	chyh toh dah • leh • koh stohnt
Where is/are…?	**Gdzie jest/są…?**
	gdj'yeh yehst/sohm…
the ticket office	**kasa biletowa**
	kah • sah bee • leh • toh • vah
the information desk	**informacja**
	een • fohr • mah • tsyah
luggage lockers/ baggage room	**skrytki bagażowe/przechowalnia bagażu**
	skryht • kee bah • gah • zhoh • veh/ psheh • hoh • vahl • n'yah bah • gah • zhoo
the platforms	**perony**
	peh • roh • nyh

For Asking Directions, see page 64.

Can I have a schedule [timetable]?	**Czy mogę prosić rozkład jazdy?**
	chyh moh • geh proh • sh'eech'
	rohs • kwaht yahz • dyh
How long is the trip [journey]?	**Jak długo trwa podróż?**
	yahk dwoo • goh trfah poh • droosh
Do I have to change trains?	**Czy muszę się przesiadać?**
	chyh moo • sheh sh'yeh psheh • sh'yah • dahch'
Do I need a reservation for this train?	**Muszę kupować miejscówkę?**
	moo • sheh koo • poh • vahch' myehys • tsoof • keh

For Tickets, see page 45.

Poland has a well-developed train network operated by state-owned **PKP (Polskie Koleje Państwowe)** and some regional operators (e.g. **Tanie Linie Kolejowe, TLK**, and **Koleje Mazowieckie, KM**). Train travel within Poland is relatively cheap. Fares differ according to the route, type of train and seating class you select. Trains that require seat reservations display the letter **R** on both the schedule and the car. You can buy tickets at the train station's ticket office or at an Orbis travel agency. It is also possible to buy tickets on the train for an additional fee. Tickets for **InterCity,** express trains and **TLK** trains are also available on the internet (www.pkp.pl). If you need a reservation, your ticket will be automatically sold with **miejscówka**, the reservation component, subject to extra charge.

YOU MAY SEE...

PERONY	platforms
INFORMACJA	information
REZERWACJE	reservations
PRZYJAZDY	arrivals
ODJAZDY	departures
KASA BILETOWA (CZYNNA/ NIECZYNNA)	ticket office (open/closed)
ROZKŁAD JAZDY	schedule [timetable]
WYJŚCIE (EWAKUACYJNE)	(emergency) exit
TOALETY	restroom [toilet]
POSTÓJ TAKSÓWEK	taxi stand
BIURO RZECZY ZNALEZIONYCH	lost-and-found [lost property office]

DEPARTURES

Which track [platform] does the train to…leave from?	**Z którego toru [peronu] odjeżdża pociąg do…?** *sktoo • reh • goh toh • roo [peh • roh • noo] ohd • yehzh • djah poh • ch'yohnk doh…*
Is this the right track [platform] for…?	**Czy to z tego toru [peronu] odjeżdża pociąg do…?** *chyh toh steh • goh toh • roo [peh • roh • noo] ohd • yehzh • djah poh • ch'yohnk doh…*
Where is track [platform]…?	**Gdzie jest tor [peron]…?** *gdj'yeh yehst tohr [peh • rohn]…*
Where do I change for…?	**Gdzie mam się przesiąść na pociąg do…?** *gdj'yeh mahm sh'yeh psheh • sh'yohn'sh'ch' nah poh • ch'yonk doh…*

YOU MAY HEAR…

Proszę wsiadać! *proh • sheh fsh'yah • dahch'*	All aboard!
Proszę bilety do kontroli. *proh • shehbee • leh • tyh doh kohn • troh • lee*	Tickets, please.
Następna stacja… *nahs • tehmp • nah stahts • yah…*	Next stop…
Musi pan się przesiąść w… *moo • sh'ee pahn sh'yeh psheh • sh'yohn'sh'ch' v…*	You have to change at…

ON BOARD

Is this seat free?	**Czy to miejsce jest wolne?**
	chyh toh myehys • tseh yehst vohl • neh
That's my seat.	**To moje miejsce.**
	toh moh • yeh myehys • tseh

BUS

Where's the bus station?	**Gdzie jest dworzec autobusowy?**
	gdj'yeh yehst dvoh • zhehts ahw • toh • boo • soh • vyh
Is it far from here?	**Czy to daleko stąd?**
	chyh toh dah • leh • koh stohnt
How do I get to…?	**Jak dojechać do…?**
	yahk doh • yeh • hahch' doh…
Does this bus stop at…?	**Czy ten autobus zatrzymuje się w…?**
	chyh tehn ahw • toh • boos zah • tshyh • moo • yeh sh'yeh v…
Could you tell me when to get off?	**Czy może mi pan powiedzieć, kiedy wysiąść?**
	chyh moh • zhe mee pahn poh • vyeh • dj'yehch' kyeh • dyh vyh • sh'on'sh'ch'
Do I have to change buses?	**Czy muszę się przesiadać?**
	chyh moo • sheh sh'yeh psheh • sh'yah • dahch'
Stop here, please!	**Proszę się zatrzymać!**
	proh • sheh sh'yeh zaht • shyh • mahch'

For Tickets, see page 45.

SUBWAY

Bus service in Poland is extensive. **PKS (Przedsiębiorstwo Komunikacji Samochodowej)** offers the widest range of routes; **Polski Express** also has numerous national routes. You can buy tickets for **PKS** buses at the bus station ticket office or from the driver. Tickets for **Polski Express** buses can be bought at bus stations or at special ticket offices in towns.

YOU MAY SEE...

PRZYSTANEK AUTOBUSOWY	bus stop
OTWIERANIE DRZWI PRZYCISKIEM	press to open door
SKASUJ BILET	validate your ticket
HAMULEC BEZPIECZEŃSTWA	emergency brake
KASOWNIK	validation machine
WYJŚCIE AWARYJNE	emergency exit

Where's the nearest metro [underground] station?
Gdzie jest najbliższa stacja metra?
gdj'yeh yehst nahy • bleesh • shah stahts • yah meht • rah

Where can I find a metro map?
Gdzie mogę znaleźć mapę metra?
gdj'yeh moh • geh znah • lesh'ch' mah • peh meht • rah

Which metro goes in the direction of...?
Które metro jedzie w stronę...?
ktoo • reh meht • roh yeh • dj'yeh fstroh • neh...

Do I have to transfer [change]? **Czy muszę się przesiadać?**
chyh moo • sheh sh'yeh psheh • sh'yah • dahch'

Is this the metro / train to...? **Czy to metro jedzie do...?**
chyh toh meht • roh yeh • dj'yeh doh...

Where are we? **Gdzie jesteśmy?**
gdj'yeh yehs • tehsh' • myh

Tickets for the metro and trams should be bought before boarding from kiosks or local shops. On boarding you must validate your ticket in a **kasownik** (validation machine). Unvalidated tickets result in an on-the-spot fine. Different types of tickets are used in different cities, but usually single-trip tickets and multiple-trip travelcards are available. In some cities electronic cards are available as well.

BOAT & FERRY

When is the ferry to...? **Kiedy odpływa prom do...?**
kyeh • dyh oht • pwyh • vah prohm doh...

Can I take my car? **Czy mogę zabrać na pokład mój samochód?**
chyh moh • geh zahb • rahch' nah pohk • wahd mooy sah • moh • hoot

What time is the next sailing? **O której jest następny rejs?**
oh ktoo • rehy yehst nahs • tehm • pnyh reyhs

Can I book a seat/cabin?	**Chciałbym** *m*/ **Chciałabym** *f* **zarezerwować miejsce siedzące/kabinę.** hch'yahw • byhm/hch'yah • wah • byhm zah • reh • zehr • _voh_ • vach' _myehys_ • tsehsh'yeh • _dzohn_ • tse/kah • _bee_ • neh
How long is the crossing?	**Jak długo trwa przeprawa?** yahk _dwoo_ • goh trfah psheh • _prah_ • vah

For Weather, see page 41.

YOU MAY SEE...

ŁODZIE RATUNKOWE	life boats
KAPOKI	life jackets
POKŁAD	deck

Regular ferry services to and from Denmark and Sweden operate from Świnoujście, Gdańsk and Gdynia. There are several ferry operators who offer various cruises on the Baltic Sea on different days of the week.

TAXI

Where can I get a taxi?	**Gdzie mogę złapać taksówkę?** gdj'yeh _moh_ • geh _zwah_ • pahch' tahk • _soof_ • keh

I'd like a taxi now/for tomorrow at…	**Chciałbym** m/**Chciałabym** f **zamówić taksówkę na jak najszybciej/na jutro na godzinę…**
	hch'yahw • byhm/hch'yah • wah • byhm zah • moo • veech' tahk • soof • keh nah yahk nahy • shyhp • ch'yehy/nah yoot • roh nah goh • dj'ee • neh…
The pick-up address is…	**Proszę mnie odebrać z…**
	proh • sheh mn'yeh oh • dehb • rahch' z…
I'm going to…	**Proszę…**
	proh • sheh…
this address	**pod ten adres**
	poht tehn ahd • rehs
the airport	**na lotnisko**
	nah loht • n'ees • koh
the train station	**na dworzec kolejowy**
	nah dvoh • zhehts koh • leh • yoh • vyh
How much?	**Ile płacę?**
	ee • leh pwah • tseh
I'm late.	**Jestem spóźniony** m/**spóźniona** f.
	yehs • tehm spoozh' • n'yoh • nyh/ spoozh' • n'yoh • nah

Can you drive faster/ slower? **Mógłby pan jechać szybciej/wolniej?**
moogw • _byh pahn_ yeh • _hahch'_
shyhp • ch'yehy/_vohl_ • n'yey

Stop/Wait here, please. **Proszę się tu zatrzymać/tu zaczekać.**
proh • _sheh sh'yeh too_
zaht • _shyh_ • mahch'/too zah • _cheh_ • kahch'

You said it would cost… **Mówił pan, że to będzie kosztowało…**
moo • veew pahn zheh toh _behn'_ • dj'yeh
kohsh • toh • _vah_ • woh…

Keep the change. **Proszę zatrzymać resztę.**
proh • sheh zah • _tshyh_ • mahch' _rehsh_ • teh

YOU MAY HEAR…

Dokąd jedziemy?   Where to?
doh • kohnt yeh • _dj'yeh_ • myh

Jaki adres?   What's the
yah • kee _ahd_ • rehs   address?

Schedule a taxi pick up by calling a local company; check the phone book for listings. You may be able to hail a taxi on the street but make sure it displays a recognized taxi company name and that the meter is started. A table of fares should be displayed in the taxi. Fares are higher on Sundays, public holidays and at night. Be careful about taking a taxi to city suburbs as it may mean entering another fare zone. Most taxis take cash only. It is not customary to tip taxi drivers.

BICYCLE & MOTORBIKE

I'd like to rent…	**Chciałbym** m/**Chciałabym** f **wynająć…**
	hch'yahw • byhm/hch'yah • wah • byhm
	vyh • nah • yohn'ch'…
a bicycle	**rower**
	roh • vehr
a moped	**motorower**
	moh • toh • roh • vehr
a motorcycle	**motor**
	moh • tohr
How much per day/ week?	**Ile kosztuje wynajęcie na dzień/ tydzień?**
	ee • leh kohsh • too • yeh
	vyh • nah • yehn' • ch'yeh nah dj'yehn'/ tyh • dj'yehn'
Can I have a helmet/ lock?	**Mogę prosić kask/blokadę?**
	moh • geh proh • sh'eech' kahsk/ bloh • kah • deh

CAR HIRE

Where can I rent a car?	**Gdzie mogę wynająć samochód?**
	gdj'yeh moh • geh vyh • nah • yohn'ch' sah • moh • hoot
I'd like to rent…	**Chcę wynająć…**
	htseh vyh • nah • yohn'ch'…
an automatic/ a manual	**samochód z automatyczną/ręczną skrzynią biegów**
	sah • moh • hoot z ahw • toh • mah • tyhch • nohm/ rehnch • nohm skshyh • n'yohm byeh • goof

a car with air conditioning	**samochód z klimatyzacją** *sah • moh • hoot sklee • mah • tyh • zahts • yohm*
a car seat	**fotelik dziecięcy** *foh • teh • leek dj'yeh • ch'yehn • tsyh*
How much…?	**Ile to kosztuje…?**

YOU MAY HEAR...

Poproszę prawo jazdy. *poh • proh • sheh prah • voh yah • zdyh*	Your driver's license, please.
Poproszę paszport. *poh • proh • sheh pahsh • pohrt*	Your passport, please.
Proszę tutaj podpisać. *proh • sheh too • tahy poht • pee • sahch'*	Please sign here.
Metta le iniziali/Firmi qui. *meht • tah leh ee • nee • tsyah • lee/ feer • mee kwee*	Initial/Sign here.

---

ee • leh toh kohsh • too • yeh…

per day/week	**za dzień/tydzień** *zah dj'yehn'/tyh • dj'yehn'*
per kilometer	**za kilometr** *zah kee • loh • mehtr*
for unlimited mileage	**bez limitu kilometrów** *behs lee • mee • too kee • loh • meht • roof*
with insurance	**z ubezpieczeniem** *zoo • behs • pyeh • cheh • n'yehm*
Are there any discounts?	**Czy są jakieś zniżki?** *chyh sohm yah • kyehsh' zn'eezh • kee*

FUEL STATION

Where's the next gas [petrol] station?	**Gdzie jest najbliższa stacja benzynowa?** *gdj'yeh yehst nahy • bleesh • shah stah • tsyah behn • zyh • noh • vah*
Fill it up, please.	**Do pełna, proszę.** *doh pehw • nah proh • sheh*
...liters, please.	**...litrów, proszę.** *...leet • roof proh • sheh*
I'll pay in cash/ by credit card.	**Zapłacę gotówką/kartą kredytową.** *zap • wah • tseh goh • toof • kohm/ kahr • tohm kreh • dyh • toh • vohm*

For Numbers, see page 20.

YOU MAY SEE...

Pb 95	regular
Pb 98	premium [super]
ON	diesel
LPG	autogas

ASKING DIRECTIONS

Is this the right road to...?	**Czy to właściwa droga do...?** *chyh toh vwahsh' • ch'ee • vah droh • gah doh...*
How far is it to...?	**Jak daleko jest stąd do...?** *yahk dah • leh • koh yehst stohnt doh...*
Where's...?	**Gdzie jest...?** *gdj'yeh yehst...*
...Street	**ulica...** *oo • lee • tsah...*

this address	**ten adres**
	tehn ahd • rehs
the highway [motorway]	**autostrada**
	ahw • toh • strah • dah
Can you show me on the map?	**Czy może mi pan pokazać na mapie?**
	chyh moh • zheh mee pahn
	poh • kah • zahch' nah mah • pyeh
I'm lost.	**Zgubiłem** *m*/**Zgubiłam** *f* **się.**
	zgoo • bee • wehm/zgoo • bee • wahm

YOU MAY HEAR...

Proszę jechać...	You should go...
proh • sheh yeh • hahch'...	
prosto	straight
prohs • toh	
w lewo	left
vleh • voh	
w prawo	right
fprah • voh	
na północ/południe	north/south
nah poow • nohts/ poh • wood • n'yeh	
na wschód/zachód	east/west
na fs • hoot/zah • hoot	
To jest...	It's...
toh yehst...	
na rogu/za rogiem	on/around the corner
nah roh • goo/zah roh • gyehm	
naprzeciwko...	opposite...
nah psheh • ch'eef • koh...	
za...	behind...
zah...	
przy...	next to...
pshyh...	

YOU MAY SEE...

	DROGA JEDNOKIERUNKOWA	one way
	DROGA Z PIERWSZEŃSTWEM	right of way
	PRZEJŚCIE DLA PIESZYCH	pedestrian crossing
STOP	**STOP**	stop
	ZAKAZ PARKOWANIA	no parking
	ZAKAZ WJAZDU	no entry
	ZAKAZ WYPRZEDZANIA	passing prohibited
	ZAKAZ ZAWRACANIA	no U-turn

PARKING

Can I park here?	**Czy mogę tu zaparkować?**
	chyh <u>moh</u> • geh too zah • pahr • <u>koh</u> • vahch'
Where is the nearest parking lot [car park]?	**Gdzie jest najbliższy parking?**
	gdj'yeh yehst nahy • <u>bleesh</u> • shyh pahr • keenk nahy • <u>bleesh</u> • shyh pahr • keenk
How much...?	**Ile kosztuje...?**
	<u>ee</u> • leh kohsh • <u>too</u> • yeh...
per hour	**godzina**
	goh • <u>dj'ee</u> • nah

per day	**dzień**
	dj'yehn'
for overnight	**zostawienie samochodu na noc**
	zohs • tah • vyeh • n'yeh
	sah • moh • hoh • doo nah nohts

BREAKDOWN & REPAIR

My car broke down/ won't start.	**Mój samochód się zepsuł/nie chce zapalić.**
	mooy sah • moh • hoot sh'yeh zehp • soow/ n'yeh htsehzah • pah • leech'
Can you fix it (today)?	**Możecie to naprawić (dzisiaj)?**
	moh • zheh • ch'yeh toh nahp • rah • veech' (dj'ee • sh'yahy)
When can I pick up the car?	**Kiedy mogę odebrać samochód?**
	kyeh • dyh moh • geh oh • dehb • rahch' sah • moh • hoot
How much?	**Ile to kosztuje?**
	ee • leh toh kohsh • too • yeh

For Time, see page 24.

ACCIDENTS

There was an accident.	**Był wypadek.**
	byhw vyh • pah • dehk
Call an ambulance/ the police.	**Proszę wezwać karetkę/policję.**
	proh • sheh vehz • vahch' kah • reht • keh/ poh • leets • yeh

For Police, see page 140.

NEED TO KNOW

Can you recommend a hotel?	**Czy może mi pan polecić jakiś hotel?** *chyh <u>moh</u> • zheh mee pahn poh • <u>leh</u> • ch'eech' yah • keesh' <u>hoh</u> • tehl*
I have a reservation.	**Mam rezerwację.** *mahm reh • zehr • <u>vahts</u> • yeh*
My name is…	**Nazywam się…** *nah • <u>zyh</u> • vahm sh'yeh…*
I would like a room…	**Chciałbym** m/**Chciałabym** f **wynająć pokój…** *<u>hch'yahw</u> • byhm/<u>hch'yah</u> • wah • byhm vyh • <u>nah</u> • yohn'ch' <u>poh</u> • kooy…*
for one/two	**jednoosobowy/dwuosobowy** *yehd • noh • oh • soh • <u>boh</u> • vyh/ dvoo • oh • soh • <u>boh</u> • vyh*
with a bathroom	**z łazienką** *zwah • <u>zh'yehn</u> • kohm*

with air conditioning	**z klimatyzacją**
	sklee • mah • tyh • <u>zahts</u> • yohm
For…	**Na…**
	nah…
tonight	**tę noc**
	teh nohts
two nights	**dwie noce**
	dvyeh <u>noh</u> • tseh
one week	**tydzień**
	<u>tyh</u> • dj'yehn'
How much?	**Ile to kosztuje?**
	<u>ee</u> • leh toh kohsh • <u>too</u> • yeh
Do you have anything cheaper?	**Czy są jakieś tańsze pokoje?**
	chyh sohm <u>yah</u> • kyehsh' <u>tahn'</u> • sheh poh • <u>koh</u> • yeh
When's check-out?	**O której mamy zwolnić pokój?**
	oh <u>ktoo</u> • rehy <u>mah</u> • myh <u>zvohl</u> • n'eech' <u>poh</u> • kooy
Can I leave this in the safe?	**Mogę zostawić to w sejfie?**
	moh • geh zohs • <u>tah</u> • veech' toh <u>fsehy</u> • fyeh
Can I leave my luggage?	**Mogę zostawić mój bagaż?**
	<u>moh</u> • geh zohs • <u>tah</u> • veech' mooy <u>bah</u> • gahsh
Can I have the bill/ a receipt?	**Czy mogę prosić o rachunek/ pokwitowanie?**
	chyh <u>moh</u> • geh <u>pro</u> • sh'eech' oh rah • <u>hoo</u> • nehk/ poh • kfee • toh • <u>vah</u> • n'yeh
I'll pay in cash/ by credit card.	**Zapłacę gotówką/kartą kredytową.**
	zah • <u>pwah</u> • tseh goh • <u>toof</u> • kohm/ <u>kahr</u> • tohm kreh • dyh • <u>toh</u> • vohm

SOMEWHERE TO STAY

Can you recommend a hotel?	**Czy może mi pan polecić jakiś hotel?** *chyh moh • zheh mee pahn* *poh • leh • ch'eech' yah • keesh' hoh • tehl*
What is it near?	**Koło czego on się znajduje?** *koh • woh cheh • goh ohn sh'yeh* *znahy • doo • yeh*
How do I get there?	**Jak można się tam dostać?** *yahk mohzh • nah sh'yeh tahm* *dohs • tahch'*

i

If you have nowhere to stay booked on arrival, visit
the local **Informacja Turystyczna** (Tourist Information Office)
for recommendations on places to stay. These are usually
located in the city center and/or near the train station.

AT THE HOTEL

I have a reservation.	**Mam rezerwację.** *mahm reh • zehr • vahts • yeh*
My name is…	**Nazywam się…** *nah • zyh • vahm sh'yeh…*
I would like a room…	**Chciałbym** m/**Chciałabym** f **wynająć pokój…** *hch'yahw • byhm/hch'yah • wah • byhm* *vyh • nah • yohn'ch' poh • kooy…*
with a bathroom	**z łazienką** *zwah • zh'yehn • kohm*

with air conditioning	**z klimatyzacją** *sklee • mah • tyh • zahts • yohm*
for smokers/ non-smokers	**dla palących/niepalących** *dla pah • lohn • tsyhh/* *n'yeh • pah • lohn • tsyhh*
For…	**Na…** *nah…*
tonight	**tę noc** *teh nohts*
two nights	**dwie noce** *dvyeh noh • tseh*

Apart from the usual hotel accomodations on offer, there are many other options as to where to lay your head when in Poland. Note that in smaller towns you will mainly find lower class hotels. Other accomodations options include: Hostels: these are inexpensive, and usually offer both private and dormitory-style rooms.

Domy Turysty (guest houses): these are ideal for budget travelers and are run by the **PTTK** (Polish Tourist Country Lovers' Society) who also run **schroniska górskie** (mountain hostels). You'll find these mainly in countryside locations. Alternatively, there are many **pensjonaty** (boarding houses) and **pokoje gościnne** (rooms in private houses) available to rent in big towns and resorts, some of which can be found and booked online. In some towns you can book a room through a tourist agency, such as **Biuro Kwater Prywatnych** or **Agencja Promocji Miasta**. Note that most **pensjonaty** provide meals and/or cooking facilities. They can accommodate fewer guests than hotels but provide a friendly and cozy atmosphere.

one week	**tydzień**
	tyh • dj'yehn'
Does the hotel have...?	**Czy jest u państwa...?**
	chyh yehst oo pahn's • tfah...
a computer for guests	**komputer dla gości**
	kohm • poo • tehr dlah gohsh' • ch'ee
an elevator [a lift]	**winda**
	veen • dah
(wireless) internet service	**(bezprzewodowy) internet**
	(behs • psheh • voh • doh • vyh) een • tehr • neht
room service	**room service**
	room sehr • vees
a pool	**basen**
	bah • sehn
a gym	**siłownia**
	sh'ee • wohv • n'yah
Could I have...?	**Czy mógłbym** m/**mogłabym** f **dostać...?**
	chyh moogw • byhm/moh • gwah • byhm dohs • tahch'...
an extra bed	**dodatkowe łóżko**
	doh • daht • koh • veh woozh • koh

YOU MAY HEAR...

Poproszę pana paszport/
kartę kredytową.
poh • proh • sheh pah • nah pahsh • pohrt/
kahr • teh kreh • dyh • toh • vohm

Your passport/
credit card,
please.

Proszę wypełnić ten formularz.
proh • sheh vyh • pehw • n'eech' tehn
fohr • moo • lahsh

Please fill out
this form.

Proszę tutaj podpisać.
proh • sheh too • tahy poht • pee • sahch'

Please sign here.

a cot	**rozkładane łóżko**
	rohs • kwah • _dah_ • neh _woozh_ • koh
a crib [child's cot]	**łóżeczko dziecięce**
	woo • _zhehch_ • koh dj'yeh • _ch'yehn_ • tseh

For Numbers, see page 20.

PRICE

How much per night/ week?	**Jaka jest cena za noc/tydzień?**
	yah • kah yehst _tseh_ • nah zah nohts/ _tyh_ • dj'yehn˙
Does the price include breakfast/ sales tax [VAT]?	**Czy w cenę wliczone jest śniadanie/ wliczony jest VAT?**
	chyh f _tseh_ • neh vlee • _choh_ • neh yehst sh'n'yah • _dah_ • n'yeh/vlee • _choh_ • nyh yehst vaht

PREFERENCES

Can I see the room?	**Czy mógłbym m/mogłabym f zobaczyć ten pokój?**
	chyh _moogw_ • byhm/_moh_ • gwah • byhm zoh • _bah_ • chych' tehn _poh_ • kooy
I'd like a…room.	**Chciałbym m/Chciałabym f … pokój.**
	hch'yahw • byhm/_hch'yah_ • wah • byhm … _poh_ • kooy
better	**lepszy**
	lehp • shyh
bigger	**większy**
	vyenh • kshyh
cheaper	**tańszy**
	tahn' • shyh
quieter	**cichszy**
	_ch'ee_ • hshyh

I'll take it.	**Wezmę ten pokój**
	vehz • meh tehn poh • kooy
No, I won't take it.	**Nie, nie chcę tego pokoju**
	n'yeh, n'yeh htseh teh • goh poh • koh • yoo

QUESTIONS

Where is/are…?	**Gdzie jest/są…?**
	gdj'eh yehst/sohm…
the bar	**bar**
	bahr
the bathrooms	**toaleta**
[toilets]	*toh • ah • leh • tah*
the elevators [lifts]	**windy**
	veen • dyh
Can I have…?	**Czy mogę dostać…?**
	chyh moh • geh dohs • tahch'…
a blanket	**koc**
	kohts
an iron	**żelazko**
	zheh • lahs • koh
a pillow	**poduszkę**
	poh • doosh • keh
soap	**mydło**
	myhd • woh
toilet paper	**papier toaletowy**
	pah • pyehr toh • ah • leh • toh • vyh
a towel	**ręcznik**
	rehnch • n'eek
Do you have an	**Czy ma pan do tego przejściowkę?**
	chyh mah pahn
adapter for this?	*doh teh • goh pshehysh' • ch'yoof • keh*
How do I turn on the	**Jak się włącza światło?**
lights?	*yahk sh'yeh vwohn • chah*
	sh'fyaht • woh

YOU MAY SEE…

PCHAĆ/CIĄGNĄĆ	push/pull
TOALETA	bathrooms [toilet]
PRYSZNICE	showers
WINDY	elevators [lifts]
SCHODY	stairs
PRALNIA	laundry
NIE PRZESZKADZAĆ	do not disturb
DRZWI PRZECIWPOŻAROWE	fire door
WYJŚCIE (AWARYJNE)	(emergency) exit
BUDZENIE TELEFONICZNE	wake-up call

Please wake me at…	**Proszę mnie obudzić o…**
	proh • sheh mn'yeh
	oh • boo • dj'eech' oh…
Could I have my things from the safe?	**Mógłbym** _m_/**Mogłabym** _f_ **wyjąć moje rzeczy z sejfu?**
	moogw • byhm/moh • gwah • byhm
	vyh • yohn'ch' moh • yeh zheh • chyh
	ssehy • foo
Can I leave this in the safe?	**Czy mogę to zostawić w sejfie?**
	chyh moh • geh toh zohs • tah • veech'
	fsehy • fyeh
Is there any mail [post] for me?	**Czy są jakieś listy do mnie?**
	chyh sohm yah • kyehsh' lees • tyh doh
	mn'yeh
Are there any messages for me?	**Czy są dla mnie jakieś wiadomości?**
	chyh sohm dlah mn'yeh yah • kyehsh'
	vyah • doh • mosh' • ch'ee

Do you have a laundry service?	**Czy świadczycie Państwo usługę prania odzieży?**
	chyh sh'vyaht • chyh • ch'yeh pahn' • stvoh oo • swoo • geh prah • n'yah oh • dj'yeh • zhy

PROBLEMS

There's a problem.	**Mam problem.**
	mahm prohb • lehm
I've lost my key.	**Zgubiłem** m/**Zgubiłam** f **klucz.**
	zgoo • bee • wehm/zgoo • bee • wahm klooch
I've locked the key in my room.	**Zatrzasnąłem** m/**Zatrzasnęłam** f **klucz w pokoju.**
	zah • tshahs • noh • wehm/ zah • tshahs • neh • wahm klooch fpoh • koh • yoo
The room is dirty.	**Pokój jest brudny.**
	poh • kooy yehst brood • nyh
There are bugs in my room.	**W moim pokoju są robaki.**
	vmoh • eem poh • koh • yoo sohm roh • bah • kee
There is no hot water/ toilet paper.	**Nie ma ciepłej wody/papieru toaletowego.**
	n'yeh mah ch'yehp • wehy voh • dyh/pah • pyeh • roo toh • ah • leh • toh • veh • goh
…doesn't work.	**…nie działa.**
	…n'yeh dj'yah • wah
Can you fix…?	**Mogą państwo naprawić…?**
	moh • gohm pahn's • tfoh nahp • rah • veech'…
the air conditioning	**klimatyzację**
	klee • mah • tyh • zahts • yeh

the fan	**wentylator**
	vehn • tyh • lah • tohr
he heat [heating]	**ogrzewanie**
	oh • gzheh • vah • n'yeh
the light	**światło**
	sh'fyaht • woh
the TV	**telewizor**
	teh • leh • vee • zohr
the toilet	**toaletę**
	toh • ah • leh • teh
I'd like another room.	**Chciałbym** *m/***Chciałabym** *f* **zmienić pokój.**
	hch'yahw • byh /hch'yah • wah • byhm zmyeh • n'eech' poh • kooy

Poland's electricity is 230 volts. You may need a converter and/or an adapter for your appliance.

CHECKING OUT

When's check-out?	**O której mam zwolnić pokój?**
	oh ktoo • rehy mahm zvohl • n'eech' poh • kooy
Could I leave my bags here until…?	**Czy mogę zostawić tutaj bagaż do…?**
	chyh moh • geh zohs • tah • veech' too • tahy bah • gahsh doh…
Can I have an itemized bill/ a receipt?	**Czy mogę dostać szczegółowy rachunek/pokwitowanie?**
	chyh moh • geh dohs • tach' shcheh • goo • woh • vyh ra • hoo • nehk/ poh • kfee • toh • vah • n'yeh

I think there's a mistake in this bill.	**Na tym rachunku chyba jest błąd.** *nah tyhm rah • _hoon_ • koo hyh • bah yehst blohnt*
I'll pay in cash/by credit card.	**Zapłacę gotówką/kartą kredytową.** *zah • _pwah_ • tseh goh • _toof_ • kohm/ kahr • tohm kreh • dyh • _toh_ • vohm*

RENTING

I've reserved an apartment/a room.	**Zarezerwowałem** m/**Zarezerwowałam** f **mieszkanie/pokój.** *zah • reh • zehr • voh • _vah_ • wehm/ zah • reh • zehr • voh • vah • lahm myehsh • _kah_ • n'yeh/poh • kooy*
My name is…	**Nazywam się…** *nah • _zyh_ • vahm sh'yeh…*
Can I have the key/ key card?	**Czy mogę dostać klucz/kartę?** *chyh moh • geh dohs • tahch' klooch/ _kahr_ • teh*
Are there…?	**Czy są…?** *chyh sohm…*
dishes [crockery]	**naczynia** *nah • _chyh_ • n'yah*
pillows	**poduszki** *poh • _doosh_ • kee*
Are there…?	**Czy są/jest…?** *chyh sohm/yehst…*
sheets	**pościel** *_pohsh'_ • ch'yehl*
towels	**ręczniki** *rehnch • _n'ee_ • kee*
kitchen utensils	**sztućce** *_shtooch'_ • tseh*

When do I put out the bins?	**Kiedy wywożą śmieci?**
	kyeh • dyh vyh • voh • zhohm sh'myeh • ch'ee
…is broken.	**…nie działa.**
	…n'yeh dj'yah • wah
How does…work?	**Jak obsługiwać…?**
	yahk ohp • swoo • gee • vahch'…
the air conditioner	**klimatyzator**
	klee • mah • tyh • zah • tohr
the dishwasher	**zmywarkę**
	zmyh • vahr • keh
the freezer	**zamrażarkę**
	zahm • rah • zhahr • keh
the heater	**grzejnik**
	gzhehy • n'eek
the microwave	**mikrofalówkę**
	mee • kroh • fah • loof • keh
the refrigerator	**lodówkę**
	loh • doof • keh
the stove	**kuchenkę**
	koo • hehn • keh
the washing machine	**pralkę**
	prahl • keh

DOMESTIC ITEMS

Could I have…?	**Czy mogę dostać…?**
	chyh moh • geh dohs • tahch'…
an adapter	**przejściówkę**
	pshehysh' • ch'yoof • keh
aluminum [kitchen] foil	**folię aluminiową**
	fohl • yeh ah • loo • mee • n'yoh • vohm
a bottle opener	**otwieracz do butelek**
	oht • fyeh • rahch doh boo • teh • lehk

a broom	**zmiotkę**
	zmyoht • keh
a can opener	**otwieracz do puszek**
	oht • fyeh • rahch doh poo • shehk
a corkscrew	**korkociąg**
	kohr • koh • ch'yohnk
bin bags	**worki na śmieci**
	vohr • kee nah sh'myeh • ch'ee
matches	**zapałki**
	zah • pahw • kee
a mop	**mopa**
	moh • pah
napkins	**serwetki**
	sehr • veht • kee
paper towels	**papierowe ręczniki**
	pah • pyeh • roh • veh rehnch • n'ee • kee
plastic wrap [cling film]	**folię do żywności**
	fohl • yeh doh zhyhv • nohsh' • ch'ee
a plunger	**przepychacz**
	psheh • pyh • hahch
scissors	**nożyczki**
	noh • zhyhch • kee
a vacuum cleaner	**odkurzacz**
	oht • koo • zhahch

AT THE HOSTEL

Do you have any places left for tonight?	**Czy są na dzisiaj wolne miejsca?**
	chyh sohm nah dj'ee • sh'yahy vohl • neh myehys • tsah
I would like a single/ double room.	**Chciałbym m/Chciałabym f pokój jednoosobowy/dwuosobowy.**
	hch'yahw • byhm/hch'yah • wah • byhm poh • kooy yehd • noh • oh • soh • boh • vyh/ dvoo • oh • soh • boh • vyh

Could I have...?	**Czy mógłbym _m_/mogłabym _f_ dostać...?**
	chyh moogw • byhm/moh • gwah • byhm dohs • tahch'...
a blanket	**koc**
	kohts
a pillow	**poduszkę**
	poh • doosh • keh
sheets	**pościel**
	pohsh' • ch'yehl
a towel	**ręcznik**
	rehnch • n'eek
Do you have lockers?	**Czy są tu zamykane schowki?**
	Chyh sohm too zah • myh • kah • neh s • hohv • kee
When do you lock up?	**O której zamykają państwo drzwi?**
	oh ktoo • rehy zah • myh • kah • yohm pahn' • stfoh djvee
Do I need a membership card?	**Czy potrzebuję karty członkowskiej?**
	Chyh poh • tsheh • boo • yeh kahr • tyh chwohn • kohv • skyehy
Here's my international student card.	**Oto moja międzynarodowa karta studencka.**
	oh • toh moh • yah myehn • dzyh • nah • roh • doh • vah kahr • tah stoo • dehn • tskah

GOING CAMPING

Can I camp here?	**Mogę tutaj rozbić namiot?**
	moh • geh too tahy rohz • beech' nah • myoht
Is there a campsite near here?	**Czy jest tu w pobliżu jakiś camping?**
	chyh yehst too fpoh • blee • zhoo yah • keesh' kehm • peenk

What is the charge per day/week?	**Ile kosztuje jedna noc/tydzień?** _ee • leh kosh • too • yeh yehd • nah nohts/ tyh • dj'yehn'_
Are there …?	**Czy są/jest?** _chyh sohm/yehst_
electric outlets	**gniazdka elektryczne** _gn'yahs • tkah eh • lehk • tryh • chneh_
showers	**prysznice** _pryhsh • n'ee • tseh_
laundry facilities	**pralnia** _prahl • n'yah_
tents for hire	**namioty do wynajęcia** _nah • myoh • tyh doh vyh • nah • yehn • ch'yah_
Where can I empty the chemical toilet?	**Gdzie mogę opróżnić chemiczną toaletę?** _gd'yeh moh • geh ohp • roozh • n'eech' heh • meech • nohm toh • ah • leh • teh_

For In the Kitchen, see page 186.

YOU MAY SEE...

WODA PITNA	potable water
ZAKAZ BIWAKOWANIA	no camping
ZAKAZ ROZPALANIA GRILLA I OGNISK	no fires or barbecues
ZAKAZ WSTĘPU	no trespassing

COMMUNICATIONS

NEED TO KNOW

Is there an internet **kafejka** cafe nearby?	**Czy jest tu gdzieś w pobliżu internetowa?** *chyh yehst too gj'yehsh' fpoh • blee • zhoo kah • fehy • kah een • tehr • neh • toh • vah*
Can I access the internet/check e-mails?	**Można tu skorzystać z internetu/ sprawdzić pocztę?** *mohzh • nah too skoh • zhyhs • tahch' zeen • tehr • neh • too/sprahw • dj'eech' pohch • teh*
How much per hour/ half hour?	**Ile kosztuje godzina/pół godziny?** *ee • leh koh • shtoo • yeh goh • dj'ee • nah/poow goh • dj'ee • nyh*
How do I connect/ log on?	**Jak mam się połączyć z siecią/ zalogować?** *yahk mahm sh'yeh poh • wohn • chyhch' ssh'yeh • ch'yohm/zah • loh • goh • vahch'*
Is there a password?	**Jest jakieś hasło?** *yehst yah • kyehsh' hahs • woh*
A phone card, please.	**Poproszę kartę telefoniczną.** *poh • proh • sheh kahr • teh teh • leh • foh • n'eech • nohm*
Can I have your phone number?	**Czy mogę prosić pana numer telefonu?** *chyh moh • geh proh • sh'eech' pah • nah noo • mehr teh • leh • foh • noo*

Here's my number/ e-mail address.	**To jest mój numer telefonu/adres e-mail.**
	toh yehst mooy <u>noo</u> • mehr teh • leh • <u>foh</u> • noo/<u>ahd</u> • rehs <u>ee</u> • mehyl
Can you call me please/e-mail me?	**Czy mógłby pan do mnie zadzwonić/ napisać do mnie maila?**
	chyh <u>moogw</u> • byh pahn doh mn'yeh zahdz • <u>voh</u> • n'eech'/nah • <u>pee</u> • sahch' doh mn'yeh <u>mehy</u> • lah
Hello. This is…	**Dzień dobry. Mówi…**
	dj'yehn' <u>dohb</u> • ryh <u>moo</u> • vee…
I'd like to speak to…	**Chciałbym** m/**Chciałabym** f **rozmawiać z…**
	hch'yahw • byhm/hch'yah • wah • byhm rohz • <u>mah</u> • vyahch' z…
Could you repeat that?	**Może pan powtórzyć?**
	<u>moh</u> • zheh pahn pohf • <u>too</u> • zhyhch'
I'll call back later.	**Zadzwonię później.**
	zahdz • <u>voh</u> • n'yeh poozh' • n'yehy
Bye.	**Do widzenia.**
	doh vee • <u>dzeh</u> • n'yah
Where's the post office?	**Gdzie jest poczta?**
	Gdj'yeh yehst <u>pohch</u> • tah
I'd like to send this to…	**Chciałbym** m/**Chciałabym** f **to wysłać do…**
	hch'yahw • byhm/hch'yah • wah • byhm toh <u>vyhs</u> • wahch' doh…

ONLINE

Is there an internet cafe nearby?	**Czy jest tu gdzieś w pobliżu kafejka internetowa?** *chyh yehst too gdj'yehsh' fpoh • blee • zhoo kah • fehy • kah een • tehr • neh • toh • vah*
Does it have wireless internet?	**Jest tam bezprzewodowy internet?** *yehst tahm behs • psheh • voh • doh • vyh een • tehr • neht*
What is the WiFi password?	**Jakie jest hasło do sieci WiFi?** *yah • kyeh yehst hahs • woh doh sh'yeh • ch'ee vee phee*
Is the WiFi free?	**Czy korzystanie z WiFi jest bezpłatne?** *chyh koh • zhy • stah • nyeh z vee phee yehst behs • pwaht • neh*
Do you have bluetooth?	**masz funkcję Bluetooth?** *mahsh foon • ktsyeh bloo • tooth*
How do I turn the computer on/off?	**Jak włączyć/wyłączyć komputer?** *yak vwohn • chyhch'/wyh • wohn • chyhch' kohm • poo • tehr*
How much per hour/ half hour?	**Ile kosztuje godzina/pół godziny?** *ee • leh kohsh • too • yeh goh • dj'ee • nah/ poow goh • dj'ee • nyh*
Can I...?	**Mogę...?** *moh • geh...*
access the internet	**skorzystać z internetu** *skoh • zhyhs • tahch' zeen • tehr • neh • too*
check e-mail	**sprawdzić pocztę** *sprahv • dj'eech' pohch • teh*
print something	**coś wydrukować** *tsohsh' vyh • droo • koh • vahch'*
access Skype?	**używać Skype'a?** *ooh • zhyh • vahch' skahy • pah*

plug in/charge my laptop/iPhone/ iPad/BlackBerry?	**podłączyć/naładować laptopa/ iPhone'a/iPada/Blackberry?** *pohd • wohn • chyhch'/ nah • wah • doh • vach' lahp • toh • pah/ ahy • foh • nah/ahy • pah • dah/ blahk • beh • ryh*
How do I...?	**Jak mam się...?** *yahk mahm sh'yeh...*
connect/ disconnect	**połączyć z siecią/rozłączyć** *poh • wohn • chyhch' ssh'yeh • ch'yohm/ rohz • wohn • chyhch'*
log on/off	**zalogować/wylogować** *zah • loh • goh • vahch'/ wyh • loh • goh • vahch'*

YOU MAY SEE...

ZAMKNIJ	close
USUŃ	delete
E-MAIL	e-mail
ZAKOŃCZ	exit
POMOC	help
KOMUNIKATOR	instant messenger
ZALOGUJ SIĘ	login
ANULUJ	cancel
OTWARTE	open
DRUKUJ	print
ZAPISZ	save
NAZWA UŻYTKOWNIKA	username
HASŁO	password
(BEZPRZEWODOWY) INTERNET	(wireless) internet

How do I type this symbol?	**Jak wpisać ten symbol?**
	yahk fpee • sahch' tehn syhm • bohl
What's your e-mail?	**Jaki jest pana adres e-mail?**
	yah • kee yehst pah • nah ahd • rehs ee • mehyl
My e-mail is…	**Mój e-mail to…**
	mooy ee • meyhl toh…
Do you have a scanner?	**Czy jest tu skaner?**
	Chyh yehst too skah • nehr

SOCIAL MEDIA

Are you on Facebook/Twitter?	**Masz konto na Facebooku/Twitterze?**
	mahsh kohn • toh nah fehys • boo • koo/ twee • teh • zheh
What's your username?	**Pod jaką nazwą masz konto?**
	pohd yah • kohm nahz • vohm mahsh kohn • toh
I'll add you as a friend.	**Dodam Cię do znajomych.**
	doh • dahm ch'yeh doh znah • yoh • myhh
I'll follow you on Twitter.	**Będę śledził/śledziła twoje wpisy na Twitterze.**
	behn • deh sh'leh • 'dj'eewh/ sh'leh • 'dj'ee • wah tfoh • yeh fpee • syh nah twee • teh • zheh
Are you following…?	**Czy śledzisz wpisy….?**
	chyh sh'leh • dj'eesh fpee • syh…
I'll put the pictures on Facebook/Twitter.	**Wrzucę zdjęcia na Facebooka/Twittera.**
	vzhoo • tseh zdyehn • chy'ahh nah fehys • boo • kah/twee • teh • rah
I'll tag you in the pictures.	**Zaznaczę cię na zdjęciach.**
	zah • znah • cheh ch'yeh nah zdyehn • chy'ahh

PHONE

A phone card, please.	**Poproszę kartę telefoniczną.** *poh • proh • sheh kahr • teh* *teh • leh • foh • n'eech • nohm*
How much?	**Ile to kosztuje?** *ee • leh toh kohsh • too • yeh*
My phone doesn't work here.	**Mój telefon tu nie działa.** *mooy teh • leh • fohn too n'yeh dj'yah • wah*
What's the country code for…?	**Jaki jest numer kierunkowy do…?** *yah • kee yehst noo • mehr* *kyeh • roon • koh • vyh doh…*
What's the number for Information?	**Jaki jest numer do informacji?** *yah • kee yehst noo • mehr doh* *een • fohr • mahts • yee*
I'd like the number for…	**Proszę o numer telefonu do…** *proh • sh'eh oh noo • mehr* *teh • leh • foh • noo doh…*
My phone doesn't work here.	**Mój telefon tu nie działa.** *mooy teh • leh • fohn too n'yeh dj'yah • wah*
What network are you on?	**W jakiej jesteś sieci?** *vyah • kyey yehs • tehsh' sh'yeh • ch'ee*
Is it 3G?	**Czy jest to sieć 3G?** *tchyh yehst toh shy'ech' tshyh gyeh*
I have run out of credit/minutes.	**Skończyła mi się karta.** *skohn' • chyh • wah mee sh'yeh kahr • tah*
Can I buy some credit?	**Czy mogę tu doładować kartę?** *tchyh moh • geh tooh* *doh • wah • doh • vahch' kahr • teh*
Do you have a phone charger?	**Czy ma Pan m/Pani f ładowarkę do telefonu?** *chyh mah pahn/ pahnee* *wah • doh • vahr • keh doh* *teh • leh • foh • noo*

Can I have your phone number?	**Czy mogę dostać twój numer telefonu?**
	chyh moh•geh doh•stahch' tfooy noo•mehr teh•leh •foh•noo
Here's my number.	**Oto mój numer telefonu.**
	oh •toh mooy noo•mehr teh•leh •foh•noo
Please call/text me.	**Zadzwoń do mnie/przyślij mi SMS.**
	zah •dzvohn' doh mnyeh/pshyh•sh'leey mee ehs•ehm•ehs
I'll call/text you.	**Zadzwonię do ciebie/wyślę ci SMS.**
	zah •dzvoh•n'yeh doh ch'yeh •byeh/ vyh•sh'leh ch'ee ehs•ehm•ehs

For Numbers, see page 20.

TELEPHONE ETIQUETTE

Hello. This is…	**Dzień dobry. Mówi…**
	dj'yen' dohb•ryh moo•vee…
I'd like to speak to…	**Chciałbym** m/**Chciałabym** f **rozmawiać z…**
	hch'yahw•byhm/hch'yah •wah•byhm rohz•mah•vyahch' z…
Extension…	**Wewnętrzny…**
	vehv•nehntsh•nyh…
Speak louder/more slowly, please.	**Proszę mówić głośniej/wolniej.**
	proh •sh'eh moo•veech' gwohsh'•n'yehy/ vohl•n'yehy
Could you repeat that?	**Mógłby pan powtórzyć?**
	moogw•byh pahn pohf•too•zhyhch'
I'll call back later.	**Zadzwonię później.**
	zahdz•voh •n'yeh poozh'•n'yehy
Bye.	**Do widzenia.**
	doh vee•dzeh •n'yah

Public phones are card operated. A local or international **karta telefoniczna** (phone card) can be purchased from kiosks or post offices. Be sure to break off the perforated corner before inserting the card into the phone.

YOU MAY HEAR…

Halo.   Hello.
hah • loh
Przepraszam, kto mówi?   Who's calling,
psheh • prah • shahm ktoh moo • vee   please?
Proszę poczekać.   Please hold.
proh • sheh poh • cheh • kahch'
Przełączę pana.   I'll put you
psheh • wohn • cheh pah • nah   through.
Nie może teraz podejść.   He/She can't
n'yeh moh • zheh teh • rahs poh • deysh'ch'   come to the
                                                 phone.
Coś przekazać?   Would you like
tsohsh' psheh • kah • zahch'   to leave a
                                                 message?
Czy może do pana oddzwonić?   Can he/she call
chyh moh • zheh doh pah • nah   you back?
ohd • dzvoh • n'eech'
Jaki jest pana numer telefonu?   What's your
yah • kee yehst pah • nah noo • mehr   number?
teh • leh • foh • noo

FAX

Can I send/receive a fax here?	**Czy mogę stąd wysłać/tu odebrać faks?**
	chyh moh • geh stohnt vyhs • wahch'/too oh • dehb • rahch' fahks
What's the fax number?	**Jaki jest numer faksu?**
	yah • kee yehst noo • mehr fahk • soo
Please fax this to…	**Proszę to przefaksować do…**
	proh • sheh toh psheh • fahk • soh • vahch' doh…

POST

Where's the post office/mailbox [postbox]?	**Gdzie jest poczta/skrzynka pocztowa?**
	gdj'yeh yehst pohch • tah/skshyhn • kah pohch • toh • vah
A stamp for this postcard/letter, please.	**Poproszę znaczek na tę pocztówkę/ten list.**
	poh • proh • sheh znah • chehk nah teh pohch • toof • keh/tehn leest
How much?	**Ile to kosztuje?**
	ee • leh toh kohsh • too • yeh

YOU MAY HEAR…

Proszę wypełnić deklarację celną.
proh • sheh vyh • pehw • n'eech' deh • klah • rahts • yeh tsehl • nohm

Please fill out the customs declaration form.

Jaka jest wartość przesyłki?
yah • kah yehst wahr • tohsh'ch' psheh • syhw • kee

What's the value of the package?

Co jest w środku?
tsoh yehst fsh'roht • koo

What's inside?

I want to send this package by airmail/ express mail.	**Chcę wysłać tę paczkę pocztą lotniczą/ priorytetem.** *htseh vyhs • wahch' teh pahch • keh pohch • tohm loht • n'ee • chohm/ pryoh • ryh • teh • tehm*
A receipt, please.	**Poproszę paragon.** *poh • proh • sheh pah • rah • gohn*

> **Poczta** (the post office) has locations throughout Poland. It handles mail and provides courier, phone and fax services. Stamps and postcards can be bought at the post office and at some kiosks. Mailboxes are red and display the logo **Poczta Polska**.

SIGHTSEEING

NEED TO KNOW

Where's the tourist information office?	**Gdzie jest biuro informacji turystycznej?** *gdj'yeh yehst byoo • roh een • fohr • mah • tsyee too • ryhs • tych • nehy*
What are the main points of interest?	**Co tu warto zobaczyć?** *tsoh too vahr • toh zoh • bah • chych'*
Are there tours in English?	**Czy są wycieczki po angielsku?** *chyh sohm vyh • ch'yech • kee poh ahn • gyehl • skoo*
Can I have a map/ guide please?	**Czy mogę prosić mapę/przewodnik?** *chyh moh • geh proh • sh'eech' mah • peh/ psheh • vohd • n'eek*

While visiting Poland, tourists can enjoy arts and culture throughout the year. Classical music enthusiasts should visit Chopin's birthplace, Żelazowa Wola, during the summer for free outdoor concerts. Historic Cracow features many art galleries and museums, including **Muzeum Narodowe** (National Museum) and **Muzeum Czartoryskich** (Cartoryski Museum). Warsaw, Poland's capital, is home to numerous renowned theaters and concert halls, as well as one of Europe's most beautiful city parks, **Łazienki Królewskie**. During August, the beach town of Sopot entertains music lovers with its International Pop Festival.

TOURIST INFORMATION

Do you have any information on…?	**Czy ma pan jakieś informacje o…?** *chyh mah pahn <u>yah</u> • kyehsh' een • fohr • <u>mah</u> • tsyeh oh…*
Can you recommend…?	**Czy może pan polecić…?** *chyh <u>moh</u> • zheh pahn poh • <u>leh</u> • ch'eech'…*
a bus tour	**wycieczkę autobusową** *vyh • <u>ch'yehch</u> • keh ahw • toh • boo • <u>soh</u> • wohm*
a boat trip	**rejs statkiem** *rehys <u>staht</u> • kyehm*
an excursion	**wycieczkę** *vyh • <u>ch'yehch</u> • keh*
a sightseeing tour	**wycieczkę po mieście** *vyh • <u>ch'yehch</u> • keh poh <u>myehsh</u>' • ch'yeh*

For Asking Directions, see page 64.

Most cities and large towns have a tourist information office. They are usually located in the center of town; some display the sign **IT (informacja turystyczna)**. Tourist information can also be obtained from **Orbis** and **PTTK** (Polish Tourist Organization) offices.

Most bookstores and tourist offices sell road, regional and local maps. Town maps are displayed on kiosks in major squares and streets and at tourist information offices.

ON TOUR

I'd like to go on the excursion to…	**Interesuje mnie wycieczka do…** *een • teh • reh • soo • yeh mn'yeh vyh • ch'yehch • kah doh…*
When's the next tour?	**Kiedy będzie następna wycieczka?** *kyeh • dyh behn • dj'yeh nahs • tehmp • nah vyh • ch'yech • kah*
Are there tours in English?	**Czy są wycieczki po angielsku?** *chyh sohm vyh • ch'yech • kee poh ahn • gyehl • skoo*
Is there an English guide book/audio guide?	**Czy jest przewodnik/audioprzewodnik w języku angielskim?** *chyh yehst pshe • vohd/n'eek/ ahwdyoh • pshe • vohd • n'eek vyehn • zyh • koo ahn • gyehl • skyhm*
What time do we leave/return?	**O której wyruszamy/wracamy?** *oh ktoo • rehy vyh • roo • shah • myh/ vrah • tsah • myh*
We'd like to see the…	**Chcielibyśmy zobaczyć…** *hch'yeh • lee • byhsh' • myh zoh • bah • chyhch'…*

Can we stop here…?	**Czy możemy się tu zatrzymać…?**
	chyh moh • zheh • myh sh'yeh too
	zaht • shyh • mahch'…
to take photos	**żeby zrobić zdjęcia**
	zheh • byh zroh • beech' zdyehn • ch'yah
to buy souvenirs	**żeby kupić pamiątki**
	zheh • byh koo • peech' pah • myohnt • kee
to use the restrooms [toilets]	**żeby skorzystać z toalety**
	zheh • byh skoh • zhyhs • tahch'
	stoh • ah • leh • tyh
Is it disabled-accessible?	**Czy jest dostęp dla niepełnosprawnych?**
	chyh yehst dohs • tehmp dlah
	n'yeh • pehw • noh • sprahv • nyhh

For Tickets, see page 45.

SEEING THE SIGHTS

Where's …?	**Gdzie jest/są…?**
	gdj'yeh yehst/sohm
the battleground	**pole bitwy**
	poh • leh beet • fyh
the botanical garden	**ogród botaniczny**
	oh • groot boh • tah • n'eech • nyh
the castle	**zamek**
	zah • mehk
the cathedral	**katedra**
	kah • teh • drah
the church	**kościół**
	kosh' • ch'yoow
the downtown area	**centrum**
	tsehn • troom
the fountain	**fontanna**
	fohn • tahn • nah
the library	**biblioteka**
	beeb • lyoh • teh • kah

the market	**bazar**	
	bah • zahr	
the monument	**pomnik**	
	pohm • n'eek	
the museum	**muzeum**	
	moo • zeh • oom	
the old town	**stare miasto**	
	stah • reh myahs • toh	
the opera house	**opera**	
	oh • peh • rah	
the palace	**pałac**	
	pah • wahts	
the park	**park**	
	pahrk	
the ruins	**ruiny**	
	roo • ee • nyh	
the shopping area	**centrum handlowe**	
	tsehn • troom hahn • dloh • veh	
the town square	**rynek**	
	ryh • nehk	
the town hall	**ratusz**	
	rah • toosh	
Can you show me on the map?	**Czy może mi pan pokazać na mapie?**	
	chyh moh • zheh mee pahn poh • kah • zahch' nah mah • pyeh	
It's…	**To jest…**	
	toh yehst…	
amazing	**niesamowite**	
	n'yeh • sah • moh • vee • teh	
beautiful	**piękne**	
	pyehnk • neh	
boring	**nudne**	
	nood • neh	
interesting	**interesujące**	
	een • teh • reh • soo • yohn • tseh	

magnificent	**wspaniałe**
	vspah • n'yah • weh
romantic	**romantyczne**
	roh • mahn • tyhch • neh
strange	**dziwne**
	dj'eev • neh
stunning	**olśniewające**
	ohl • sh'n'yeh • vah • yohn • tseh
terrible	**okropne**
	ohk • rohp • neh
ugly	**brzydkie**
	bzhyht • kyeh
I (don't) like it.	**(Nie) Podoba mi się to.**
	(n'yeh) poh • doh • bah mee sh'yeh toh

RELIGIOUS SITES

Where's…?	**Gdzie jest…?**
	gdj'yeh yehst
the cathedral	**katedra**
	kah • teh • drah
the Catholic/	**kościół katolicki/protestancki**
	kosh' • ch'yoow
Protestant church	*kah • toh • lee • tskee/*
	proh • tehs • tahn • tskee
the mosque	**meczet**
	meh • cheht
the shrine	**kapliczka**
	kah • pleech • kah
the synagogue	**synagoga**
	syh • nah • goh • gah
What time is mass/	**O której jest msza/nabożeństwo?**
the service?	*oh ktoo • rehy yehst mshah/*
	nah • boh • zhehn' • stfoh

LEISURE TIME

SHOPPING

NEED TO KNOW

Where is the market/ mall [shopping centre]?	**Gdzie jest targ/centrum handlowe?** *gdj'yeh yehst tahrk/tsehn • troom hahn • dloh • veh*
I'm just browsing.	**Tylko się rozglądam.** *tyhl • koh sh'yeh rohz • glohn • dahm*
Can you help me?	**Czy może mi pan pomóc?** *chyh moh • zheh mee pahn poh • moots*
I'm being helped.	**Jestem już obsługiwany** m/ **obsługiwana** f. *yehs • tehm yoosh ohp • swoo • gee • vah • nyh/ ohp • swoo • gee • vah • nah*
How much is this/ that?	**Ile to/tamto kosztuje?** *ee • leh toh/tahm • toh kosh • too • yeh*
Can you show me...?	**Może mi pan pokazać...?** *moh • zheh mee pahn poh • kah • zahch'...*
This/That one, please.	**Proszę to/tamto.** *proh • sheh toh/tahm • toh*
That's all, thanks.	**To wszystko, dziękuję.** *toh fshyhs • tkoh dj'yehn • koo • yeh*
Where can I pay?	**Gdzie mogę zapłacić?** *gdj'yeh moh • geh zah • pwah • ch'eech'*
I'll pay in cash/ by credit card.	**Zapłacę gotówką/kartą kredytową.** *zah • pwah • tseh goh • toof • kohm/ kahr • tohm kreh • dyh • toh • vohm*
A receipt, please.	**Proszę paragon.** *proh • sheh pah • rah • gohn*

AT THE SHOPS

Where is/are…?	**Gdzie jest/są…?**
	gdj'yeh yehst/sohm…
When does…open/ close?	**Od/Do której czynny jest…?**
	ohd/doh ktoo • rehy chyhn • nyh yehst…
the antiques store	**antykwariat**
	ahn • tyh • kfah • ryaht
the bakery	**piekarnia**
	pyeh • kahr • n'yah
the bank	**bank**
	bahnk
the butcher shop	**sklep mięsny**
	sklehp myehn • snyh
the bookstore	**księgarnia**
	ksh'yehn • gahr • n'yah
the camera shop	**sklep fotograficzny**
	sklehp foh • toh • grah • feech • nyh
the clothing store	**sklep odzieżowy**
	sklehp oh • dj'yeh • zhoh • vyh
the delicatessen	**delikatesy**
	deh • lee • kah • teh • syh
the department store	**dom towarowy**
	dohm toh • vah • roh • vyh
the florist	**kwiaciarnia**
	kfyah • ch'yahr • n'yah
the gift shop	**sklep z upominkami**
	sklehp zoo • poh • meen • kah • mee
grocery store	**sklep spożywczy**
	sklehp spoh • zhyhf • chyh
the health food store	**sklep ze zdrową żywnością**
	sklehp zeh zdroh • vohm zhyhv • nohsh' • ch'yohm

the jeweler	**jubiler**
	yoo • bee • lehr
the liquor store	**sklep monopolowy**
[off-licence]	*sklehp moh • noh • poh • loh • vyh*
market	**bazar**
	bah • zahr
the music store	**sklep muzyczny**
	sklehp moo • zychch • nyh
the pastry shop	**cukiernia**
	tsoo • kyehr • n'yah
the pharmacy	**apteka**
[chemist]	*ahp • teh • kah*
the produce	**sklep z artykułami spożywczymi**
[grocery] store	*sklehp zahr • tyh • koo • wah • mee*
	spoh • zhyhf • chyh • mee
the shoe store	**sklep obuwniczy**
	sklehp oh • boov • n'ee • chyh
the shopping mall	**centrum handlowe**
[centre]	*tsehn • troom hahn • dloh • veh*
the souvenir store	**sklep z pamiątkami**
	sklehp spahm • yohnt • kah • mee
the sporting store	**sklep sportowy**
	sklehp spohr • toh • vyh
the supermarket	**supermarket**
	soo • pehr • mahr • keht
the tobacconist	**sklep tytoniowy**
	sklehp tyh • toh • n'yoh • vyh
the newsstand	**kiosk z gazetami**
	kyohsk zgah • zeh • tah • mee
the toy store	**sklep z zabawkami**
	sklehp zzah • bahf • kah • mee

ASK AN ASSISTANT

What are the opening hours?	**Jakie są godziny otwarcia?**
	yah • kyeh sohm goh • dj'ee • nyh
	oht • fahr • ch'yah
Where is/are...?	**Gdzie jest/są...?**
	gdj'yeh yehst/sohm...
the cashier	**kasa**
	kah • sah
the escalators	**schody ruchome**
	shoh • dyh roo • hoh • meh
the elevator [lift]	**winda**
	veen • dah
the fitting room	**przymierzalnia**
	pshyh • myeh • zhahl • n'yah
the store directory	**tablica informacyjna**
	tah • blee • tsah
	een • fohr • mah • tsyhy • nah
Can you help me?	**Czy może mi pan pomóc?**
	chyh moh • zheh mee pahn poh • moots
I'm just looking.	**Tylko się rozglądam.**
	tyhl • koh sh'yeh rohz • glohn • dahm
I'm being helped.	**Jestem już obsługiwany** m/**obsługiwana** f.
	yehs • tehm yoosh
	ohp • swoo • gee • vah • nyh/
	ohp • swoo • gee • vah • nah
Do you have...?	**Czy mają państwo...?**
	chyh mah • yohm pahn' • stfoh...
Can you show me...?	**Czy może mi pan pokazać...?**
	chyh moh • zheh mee pahn
	poh • kah • zahch'...
Can you ship/ wrap it?	**Można prosić o wysłanie/opakowanie?**
	mohzh • nah proh • sh'eech'
	oh vyh • swah • n'yeh/
	oh • pah • koh • vah • n'yeh

How much?	**Ile to kosztuje?**
	ee • leh toh kohsh • too • yeh
That's all, thanks.	**To wszystko, dziękuję.**
	toh fshyhst • koh dj'yehn • koo • yeh

For Clothing, see page 111.

YOU MAY HEAR...

Czym mogę służyć?	Can I help you?
chyhm moh • geh swoo • zhyhch'	
Chwileczkę.	One moment.
hvee • lehch • keh	
Co podać?	What would you
tsoh poh • dahch'	like?
To wszystko?	Is that all?
toh fshyhst • koh	

YOU MAY SEE...

Zamknięte/otwarte	open/closed
Przerwa śniadaniowa	closed for lunch
Przymierzalnia	fitting room
Kasa	cashier
Płatność tylko gotówką	cash only
Przyjmujemy karty kredytowe	credit cards
	accepted
Godziny otwarcia	business hours
Wyjście	exit

PERSONAL PREFERENCES

I want something…	**Chciałbym** *m* /**Chciałabym** *f* **coś…**
	hch'yahw • byhm/hch'yah • wah • byhm
	tsohsh'…
cheap/expensive	**taniego/drogiego**
	tah • n'yeh • goh/droh • gyeh • goh
larger/smaller	**większego/mniejszego**
	vyehn • ksheh • goh/mn'yehy • sheh • goh
from this region	**miejscowego**
	myehy • stsoh • veh • goh
Around…euro/złoty.	**około … euro/zloty.**
	oh • koh • woh … ehw • roh/zwoh • tyhh
Is it real/fake?	**Czy to jest prawdziwe/sztuczne?**
	chyh toh yehst prahv • dj'ee • veh/
	shtoo • chneh
Could I see this/ that?	**Czy mogę zobaczyć to/tamto?**
	chyh moh • geh zoh • bah • chyhch' toh/
	tahm • toh
That's not quite what I want.	**To nie to, czego szukam.**
	toh n'yeh toh cheh • goh
	shoo • kahm
I don't like it.	**To mi się nie podoba.**
	toh mee sh'yeh n'yeh poh • doh • bah
It's too expensive.	**To jest za drogie**
	toh yehst zah droh • gyeh
I'd like to think about it.	**Chcę się nad tym zastanowić.**
	htseh sh'yeh naht tyhm
	zahs • tah • noh • veech'
I'll take it.	**Wezmę to.**
	vehz • meh toh

PAYING & BARGAINING

How much?	**Ile to kosztuje?**
	ee • leh toh kosh • too • yeh
I'll pay in cash/	**Zapłacę gotówką/kartą kredytową/**
by credit card/	**czekiem podróżnym.**
by traveler's check.	_zah • pwah • tseh goh • toof • kohm/_
	kahr • tohm kreh • dyh • toh • vohm/
	cheh • kyehm pohd • roozh • nyhm
A receipt, please.	**Proszę paragon.**
	proh • sheh pah • rah • gohn
That's too much.	**To za drogo.**
	toh zah droh • goh
I'll give you…	**Dam panu…**
	dahm pah • noo…
I only have…zlotys.	**Mam tylko…złotych.**
	mahm tyhl • koh…zwoh • tyhh
Is that your best price?	**To najniższa cena?**
	toh nay • n'eezh • shah tseh • nah
Can you give me a	**Da mi pan zniżkę?**
discount?	_dah mee pahn zn'eezh • keh_

For Numbers, see page 20.

Cash is the preferred method of payment in stores.
Larger stores and retail chains accept major credit cards.
Travelers checks and personal checks [cheques] are not
commonly accepted in Poland.

YOU MAY HEAR...

Jak chce pan zapłacić?
yahk htseh pahn zah • pwah • ch'eech'

How are you paying?

Transakcja została odrzucona.
trahn • sahk • tsyah zoh • stah • wah ohd • zhoo • tsoh • nah

Your credit card has been declined.

Proszę o dowód tożsamości.
proh • sheh oh doh • voot tohzh • sah • moh • sh'ch'ee

ID, please.

Nie przyjmujemy kart kredytowych.
n'yeh pshyh • ymoo • yeh • myh kahrt kreh • dyh • toh • vyhh

We don't accept credit cards.

Płatność tylko gotówką.
pwaht • nohsh'ch' tyhl • koh goh • toof • kohm

Cash only, please.

MAKING A COMPLAINT

I'd like...	**Chciałbym** *m*/**Chciałabym** *f*... *hch'yahw • byhm/hch'yah • wah • byhm...*
to exchange this	**to wymienić** *toh vyh • myeh • n'eech'*
to return this	**to oddać** *toh ohd • dahch'*
a refund	**zwrot pieniędzy** *zvroht pyeh • n'ehn • dzyh*
to see the manager	**porozmawiać z kierownikiem** *poh • rohz • mah • vyahch' skyeh • rohv • n'ee • kyehm*
Here's the receipt.	**Oto paragon.** *oh • toh pah • rah • gohn*

SERVICES

Can you recommend…?	**Czy może pan polecić…?**
	chyh <u>moh</u> • zheh pahn poh • <u>leh</u> • ch'eech'…
a barber	**fryzjera męskiego**
	fryh • <u>zyeh</u> • rah mehn • <u>skyeh</u> • goh
a dry cleaner	**pralnię chemiczną**
	<u>prahl</u> • n'yeh heh • <u>meech</u> • nohm
a hairdresser	**fryzjera**
	fryh • <u>zyeh</u> • rah
a laundromat [launderette]	**pralnię samoobsługową**
	<u>prahl</u> • n'yeh sah • moh • ohp • swoo • <u>goh</u> • vohm
a nail salon	**manikiurzystkę**
	mah • nee • kyoo • <u>zhyhs</u> • tkeh
a spa	**spa**
	spah
a travel agency	**biuro podróży**
	<u>byoo</u> • roh pohd • <u>roo</u> • zhyh
Can you…this?	**Może pan to…?**
	<u>moh</u> • zheh pahn toh…
alter	**poprawić**
	poh • <u>prah</u> • veech'

clean	**wyczyścić**
	vyh • chyhsh' • ch'eech'
mend	**załatać**
	zah • wah • tahch'
press	**wyprasować**
	vyh • prah • soh • vahch'
When will it be ready?	**Na kiedy to będzie gotowe?**
	nah kyeh • dyh toh behn • dj'yeh goh • toh • veh

HAIR & BEAUTY

I'd like an appointment for today/tomorrow.	**Chciałbym** *m*/**Chciałabym** *f* **umówić się na dzisiaj/jutro.**
	hch'yahw • byhm /hch'yah • wah • byhm oo • moo • veech' sh'yeh nah dj'ee • sh'yahy/ yoot • roh
I'd like…	**Poproszę o…**
	poh • proh • sheh oh…
some color/ highlights	**trochę koloru/pasemka**
	troh • heh koh • loh • roo/pah • sehm • kah
my hair styled/ blow-dried	**ułożenie/wysuszenie włosów**
	oo • woh • zheh • n'yeh/ vyh • soo • sheh • n'yeh vwoh • soof
a haircut	**strzyżenie**
	st • shyh • zheh • n'yeh
an eyebrow/ bikini wax	**depilację brwi/bikini woskiem**
	deh • pee • lahts • yeh brvee/bee • kee • n'ee vohs • kyehm
a facial	**zabieg na twarz**
	zah • byehk nah tfahsh
a manicure/ pedicure	**manicure/pedicure**
	mah • n'ee • kyoor/peh • dee • kyoor
a (sports) massage	**masaż (sportowy)**
	mah • sash (spohr • toh • vyh)

a trim	**podcięcie włosów**
	poht • ch'yen' • ch'yeh vwoh • soof
Not too short.	**Nie za krótko**
	n'yeh zah kroot • koh
Shorter here.	**Krócej tutaj**
	kroot • tsehy too • tahy
Do you offer…?	**Czy prowadzą państwo…?**
	chyh proh • vah • dzohm pahn's • tfoh…
I'd like…	**Poproszę o…**
	poh • proh • sheh oh…
acupuncture	**akupunkturę**
	ah • koo • poon • ktoo • reh
aromatherapy	**aromaterapię**
	ah • roh • mah • teh • rah • pyeh
oxygen treatment	**terapię tlenową**
	teh • rah • pyeh tleh • noh • vohm
Is there a sauna?	**Czy jest sauna?**
	chyh yehst sahw • nah

ANTIQUES

| How old is this? | **Ile to ma lat?** |
| | *ee • leh toh mah laht* |

Throughout Poland, there are many popular health resorts of long-standing tradition such as **Busko-Zdrój**, **Konstancin Jeziorna**, **Duszniki Zdrój**, **Krynica**, **Nałęczów** and **Szczawnica** where the waters are known to have healing qualities. Spas and wellness centers, both day and overnight, can be found in large cities and seaside resorts (**Jurata**, **Jastarnia**, **Łeba**, **Sopot**, **Ustka**), the lake region (**Augustów**) and the mountains (**Zakopane**, **Bielsko-Biała**). These offer a wide range of high-quality services and are usually relatively expensive.

Do you have anything from the…period?	**Ma pan coś z okresu…?** *mah pahn tsohss' zoh • kreh • soo…*
Do I have to fill out any forms?	**Czy muszę wypełniać jakiś formularz?** *chyh moo • sheh vyh • pehw • n'yahch' yah • keess' fohr • moo • lahsh*
Is there a certificate of authenticity?	**Czy to ma świadectwo autentyczności?** *chyh toh mah sh'fyah • dehts • tfoh aw • tehn • tyhch • nohss' • ch'ee*
Can you ship/wrap it?	**Można prosić o wysłanie/opakowanie tego?** *mohzh • nah proh • sh'eech' oh vyh • swah • n'yeh/ oh • pah • koh • vah • n'yeh teh • goh*

CLOTHING

I'd like…	**Chciałbym** *m*/**Chciałabym** *f*… *hch'yahw • byhm/hch'yah • wah • byhm…*
Can I try this on?	**Czy mogę to przymierzyć?** *chyh moh • geh toh pshyh • myeh • zhyhch'*

It doesn't fit.	**To nie pasuje.**
	toh n'yeh pah • <u>soo</u> • yeh
It's too…	**To jest za…**
	toh yehst zah…
big	**duże**
	<u>doo</u> • zheh
small	**małe**
	<u>mah</u> • weh
short	**krótkie**
	<u>kroot</u> • kyeh
long	**długie**
	<u>dwoo</u> • gyeh
tight	**ciasne**
	<u>ch'yah</u> • sneh
loose	**luźne**
	<u>loo</u> • zh'neh
Do you have this in size…?	**Czy jest rozmiar…?**
	chyh yehst <u>rohz</u> • myahr…
Do you have this in a bigger/smaller size?	**Czy są większe/mniejsze rozmiary?**
	chyh sohm <u>vyehnk</u> • sheh/<u>mn'yehy</u> • sheh rohz • <u>myah</u> • ryh

---

YOU MAY SEE…

ODZIEŻ DAMSKA	men's clothing
ODZIEŻ MĘSKA	women's clothing
UBRANIA DLA DZIECI	children's clothing

YOU MAY HEAR...

Świetnie w tym pan wygląda.
<u>sh'vyeht</u> • n'yeh pahn <u>vyh</u> • <u>glohn</u> • dah

That looks great on you.

Jak to pasuje?
yahk toh pah • <u>soo</u> • yeh

How does it fit?

Nie mamy pana rozmiaru.
n'yeh mah • myh <u>pah</u> • nah rohz • <u>myah</u> • roo

We don't have your size.

COLORS

I want something…	**Chciałbym** *m*/**Chciałabym** *f* **coś w kolorze…** <u>hch'yahw</u> • byhm /<u>hch'yah</u> • wah • byhm tsohsh' fkoh • <u>loh</u> • zheh…
beige	**beżowym** beh • <u>zhoh</u> • vyhm
black	**czarnym** <u>chahr</u> • nyhm
blue	**niebieskim** n'yeh • <u>byehs</u> • keem
brown	**brązowym** brohn • <u>zoh</u> • vyhm
gray	**szarym** <u>shah</u> • ryhm
green	**zielonym** zh'yeh • <u>loh</u> • nyhm
olive	**oliwkowym** oh • leef • <u>koh</u> • vyhm
orange	**pomarańczowym** poh • mah • rahn' • <u>choh</u> • vyhm

pink	**różowym**
	roo • zhoh • vyhm
purple	**fioletowym**
	fioh • leh • toh • vyhm
red	**czerwonym**
	chehr • voh • nyhm
white	**białym**
	byah • wyhm
yellow	**żółtym**
	zhoow • tyhm

CLOTHES & ACCESSORIES

a backpack	**plecak**
	pleh • tsahk
a bag	**torba**
	tohr • bah
a belt	**pasek**
	pah • sehk
a bikini	**bikini**
	bee • kee • n'ee
a blouse	**bluzka**
	bloos • kah
a bra	**biustonosz**
	byoos • toh • nohsh
briefs [underpants]/ panties (women's)	**majtki** (for both sexes)/**slipy** (men's)/ **figi**
	mahyt • kee/ slee • pyh/ fee • gee
a coat (long/short)	**płaszcz/kurtka**
	pwahshch/koort • kah
a dress	**sukienka**
	soo • kyehn • kah
a hat	**kapelusz**
	kah • peh • loosh

a jacket	**marynarka** m/**żakiet** f
	mah • ryh • nahr • kah/zhah • kyeht
jeans	**dżinsy**
	dj'een • syh
pajamas	**piżama**
	pee • zhah • mah
pants [trousers]	**spodnie**
	spohd • n'yeh
pantyhose [tights]	**rajstopy**
	ray • stoh • pyh
a purse [handbag]	**torebka**
	toh • rehp • kah
a raincoat	**płaszcz przeciwdeszczowy**
	pwahshch
	psheh • ch'eev • dehsh • choh • vyh
a scarf	**szalik**
	shah • leek
a shirt	**koszula** m/**bluzka** f
	koh • shoo • lah /bloos • kah
shorts	**szorty**
	shohr • tyh
a skirt	**spódnica**
	spood • n'ee • tsah
socks	**skarpetki**
	skahr • peht • kee
stockings	**pończochy**
	pohn' • choh • hyh
a suit	**garnitur** m/**kostium** f
	gahr • n'ee • toor /kohs • tyoom
sunglasses	**okulary przeciwsłoneczne**
	oh • koo • lah • ryh
	psheh • ch'eef • swoh • nehch • neh
a sweater	**sweter**
	sfeh • tehr

a sweatshirt	**bluza**
	bloo • zah
swimming trunks	**kąpielówki**
	kohm • pyeh • _loof_ • kee
a swimsuit	**kostium kąpielowy**
	kohs • tyoom kohm • pyeh • _loh_ • vyh
a T-shirt	**t-shirt**
	tee • shehrt
a tie	**krawat**
	krah • vaht
underwear	**bielizna**
	byeh • _lee_ • znah

FABRIC

I'd like…	**Chciałbym** m/**Chciałabym** f **coś…**
	hch'yahw • byhm /_hch'yah_ • wah • byhm
	tsohsh'…
cotton	**z bawełny**
	zbah • _vehw_ • nyh
denim	**z dżinsu**
	zdjeen • soo
lace	**z koronki**
	skoh • _rohn_ • kee
leather	**ze skóry**
	zeh _skoo_ • ryh
linen	**z lnu**
	zlnoo
silk	**z jedwabiu**
	zyehd • _vah_ • byoo
wool	**z wełny**
	zvehw • nyh
Is it machine washable?	**Czy można to prać w pralce?**
	chyh _mohzh_ • nah toh prahch' fprahl • tseh

SHOES

I'd like…	**Chciałbym** m/**Chciałabym** f**…**
	hch'yahw • byhm /hch'yah • wah • byhm…
high-heeled/	**buty na wysokim obcasie/płaskim**
flat shoes	**obcasie**
	boo • tyh nah vyh • soh • keem
	ohp • tsah • sh'yeh/pwahs • keem
	ohp • tsah • sh'yeh
boots	**botki**
	boht • kee
loafers	**mokasyny**
	moh • kah • syh • nyh
sandals	**sandały**
	sahn • dah • wyh
shoes	**buty**
	boo • tyh
slippers	**kapcie**
	kahp • ch'yeh
sneakers	**buty sportowe**
	boo • tyh spohr • toh • veh
In size…	**Rozmiar…**
	rohz • myahr…

For Numbers, see page 20.

SIZES

small (S)	**mały/S**
	mah • wyh/ehs
medium (M)	**średni/M**
	sh'rehd • n'ee/ehm
large (L)	**duży/L**
	doo • zhyh/ehl

extra large (XL)	**bardzo duży/XL**
	bahr • dzoh <u>doo</u> • zhyh/eeks • _ehl_
petite	**rozmiar petite**
	rohz • myahr peh • <u>teet</u>
plus size	**rozmiar plus**
	rohz • myahr ploos

NEWSAGENT & TOBACCONIST

Do you sell English-language newspapers?	**Czy sprzedają państwo gazety anglojęzyczne?**
	chyh spsheh • <u>dah</u> • yohm <u>pahn'</u> • stfoh gah • <u>zeh</u> • tyh anh • gloh • yehn • <u>zyhch</u> • neh
I'd like…	**Poproszę…**
	poh • <u>proh</u> • sheh…
candy	**cukierka/batonik**
	coo • <u>kyehr</u> • kah/bah • <u>toh</u> • n'eek
chewing gum	**gumę do żucia**
	<u>goo</u> • meh doh <u>zhoo</u> • ch'yah
a chocolate bar	**tabliczkę czekolady**
	tahb • <u>leech</u> • keh cheh • koh • <u>lah</u> • dyh
a cigar	**cygaro**
	tsyh • <u>gah</u> • roh
a pack/carton of cigarettes	**paczkę/karton papierosów**
	<u>pahch</u> • keh/<u>kahr</u> • tohn pah • pyeh • <u>roh</u> • soof
a lighter	**zapalniczkę**
	zah • pahl • <u>n'eech</u> • keh
a magazine	**pismo**
	<u>pees</u> • moh
matches	**zapałki**
	zah • <u>pahw</u> • kee
a newspaper	**gazetę**
	gah • <u>zeh</u> • the

a pen	**długopis**
	dwoo • goh • pees
a postcard	**pocztówkę**
	pohcz • toof • keh
a road/town map...	**mapę drogową/miasta...**
	mah • peh droh • goh • vohm/myah • stah...
stamps	**znaczki**
	znahch • kee

PHOTOGRAPHY

I'm looking for... camera.	**Szukam...aparatu fotograficznego.**
	shoo • kahm...ah • pah • rah • too foh • toh • grah • feech • neh • goh
an automatic	**automatycznego**
	ahw • toh • mah • tyhch • neh • goh
a digital	**cyfrowego**
	tsyhf • roh • veh • goh
a disposable	**jednorazowego**
	yehd • noh • rah • zoh • veh • goh
I'd like...	**Poproszę...**
	poh • proh • sheh...
a battery	**baterię**
	bah • teh • ryeh
digital prints	**wydruki zdjęć z aparatu cyfrowego**
	vyh • droo • kee zdyehnch' zah • pah • rah • too tsyhf • roh • veh • goh
a memory card	**kartę pamięci**
	kahr • teh pah • myehn' • ch'ee
Can I print digital photos here?	**Czy mogę tu wydrukować zdjęcia z aparatu cyfrowego?**
	chyh moh • geh too vyh • droo • koh • vach' zdyehn' • ch'yah zah • pah • rah • too tsyhf • roh • veh • goh

When will the photos be ready? **Na kiedy zdjęcia będą gotowe?**
nah kyeh • dyh zdyehn' • ch'yah behn • dohm goh • toh • veh

SOUVENIRS

amber jewelry	**biżuteria z bursztynu** *bee • zhoo • teh • ryah zboor • shtyh • noo*
box of chocolates	**pudełko czekoladek/bombonierka** *poo • dehw • koh cheh • koh • lah • dehk/ bohm • boh • n'yehr • kah*
crystal	**kryształ** *kryhsh • tahw*
cut glass	**szlifowane szkło** *shlee • foh • vah • neh shkwoh*
hand-painted eggs	**pisanki** *pee • sahn • kee*
hand-painted wooden box	**ręcznie malowane drewniane pudełko** *rehnch • n'yeh mah • loh • vah • neh drehv • n'yah • neh poo • dehw • koh*
key ring	**breloczek na klucze** *breh • loh • chehk nah kloo • cheh*
Polish vodka	**polska wódka** *pohl • skah voot • kah*
postcard	**pocztówka** *pohch • toof • kah*
poster	**plakat** *plah • kaht*
silver jewelry	**biżuteria ze srebra** *bee • zhoo • teh • ryah zeh sreh • brah*
tapestry	**kilim** *kee • leem*
T-shirt	**t-shirt** *tee • shehrt*

wood carving	**figurka z drewna**
	fee • <u>goor</u> • kah <u>zdrehv</u> • nah
Could I see this/that?	**Czy mogę zobaczyć to/tamto?**
	chyh <u>moh</u> • geh zoh • <u>bah</u> • chyhch' toh/ tahm • toh
It's the one in the window/display case.	**To ten na wystawie/w gablocie.**
	toh tehn nah vyhs • <u>tah</u> • vyeh/ vgah • <u>bloh</u> • ch'yeh
I'd like…	**Chciałbym** m/**Chciałabym** f…
	<u>hch'yahw</u> • byhm/<u>hch'yah</u> • wah • byhm…
a battery	**baterię**
	bah • <u>teh</u> • ryeh
a bracelet	**bransoletkę**
	brahn • soh • <u>leht</u> • keh
a brooch	**broszkę**
	<u>brohsh</u> • keh
earrings	**kolczyki**
	kohl • <u>chyh</u> • kee
a necklace	**naszyjnik**
	nah • <u>shyhy</u> • n'eek
a ring	**pierścionek**
	pyehr • <u>sh'ch'yoh</u> • nehk
a watch	**zegarek**
	zeh • <u>gah</u> • rehk

I'd like...	**Chciałbym** m/**Chciałabym** f **coś...**
	hch'yahw • byhm /_hch'yah_ • wah • byhm tsohsh'...
amber	**z bursztynu**
	zboor • _shtyh_ • noo
copper	**z miedzi**
	zmyeh • dj'ee
crystal (quartz)	**z kryształu**
	zkryhsh • _tah_ • woo
diamond	**z brylantami**
	zbryh • lahn • _tah_ • mee
enamel	**z emalii**
	zeh • _mah_ • lee
white/yellow gold	**z białego/żółtego złota**
	z byah • _weh_ • goh/zhoow • _teh_ • goh _zwoh_ • tah
pearl	**z pereł**
	speh • rehw
pewter	**z cyny**
	s • _tsyh_ • nyh
platinum	**z platyny**
	splah • _tyh_ • nyh
silver	**ze srebra**
	zeh _sreh_ • brah
stainless steel	**ze stali nierdzewnej**
	zeh _stah_ • lee n'yeh • _rdzehv_ • nehy
Is this real?	**Czy to jest prawdziwe?**
	chyh toh yehst prahv • _dj'ee_ • veh
Can you engrave it?	**Można na tym grawerować?**
	moh • zhnah nah tyhm grah • veh • _roh_ • vach'

SPORT & LEISURE

NEED TO KNOW

Where's the game?	**Gdzie grają?**
	gdj'yeh grah • yohm
Where's…?	**Gdzie jest…?**
	gdj'yeh yehst…
the beach	**plaża**
	plah • zhah
the park	**park**
	pahrk
the pool	**basen**
	bah • sehn
Is it safe to swim/ dive here?	**Można tu bezpiecznie pływać/ skakać?**
	mohzh • nah too behs • pyehch • n'yeh pwyh • vahch'/skah • kahch'
I'd like to rent [hire] golf clubs.	**Chciałbym** *m***/Chciałabym** *f* **wypożyczyć kije golfowe.**
	hch'yahw • byhm/hch'yah • wah • byhm fvyh • poh • zhyh • chyhch' kee • yeh gohl • foh • veh
What's the charge per hour?	**Jaka jest opłata za godzinę?**
	yah • kah yehst oh • pwah • tah zah goh • dj'ee • neh
How far is it to… from here?	**Jak daleko jest stąd do…?**
	yahk dah • leh • koh yehst stohnt doh…
Can you show me on the map?	**Czy może mi pan pokazać na mapie?**
	chyh moh • zheh mee pahn poh • kah • zahch' nah mah • pyeh

WATCHING SPORT

When is…?	**Kiedy jest/są…?**
	kyeh • dyh yehst/sohm…
the basketball game	**mecz koszykówki**
	mehch koh • shyh • koof • kee
the boxing match	**zawody bokserskie**
	zah • voh • dyh bohk • sehr • skyeh
the cycling race	**wyścig rowerowy**
	vyhsh' • ch'eeg roh • veh • roh • vyh
the golf tournament	**zawody golfowe**
	zah • voh • dyh gohl • foh • veh
the soccer [football] game	**mecz piłki nożnej**
	mehch peew • kee nohzh • nehy
the tennis match	**mecz tenisowy**
	mehch teh • n'ee • soh • vyh
Who's playing?	**Kto gra?**
	ktoh grah
Where's…?	**Gdzie jest…?**
	gdj'yeh yehst…
the horsetrack	**tor wyścigów konnych**
	tohr vyhsh' • ch'ee • goof kohn • nyhh
the racetrack	**tor wyścigowy**
	tohr vyhsh' • ch'ee • goh • vyh
the stadium	**stadion**
	stah • dyohn
Where can I place a bet?	**Gdzie można postawić zakład?**
	gdj'yeh mohzh • nah pohs • tah • veech' zah • kwaht

PLAYING SPORT

Where is/are…?	**Gdzie jest/są…?**
	gdj'yeh yehst/sohm…

the golf course	**pole golfowe**
	poh • leh gohl • foh • veh
the gym	**siłownia**
	sh'ee • wohv • n'yah
the park	**park**
	pahrk
the tennis courts	**korty tenisowe**
	kohr • tyh teh • n'ee • soh • veh
How much per…?	**Jaka jest stawka za…?**
	yah • kah yehst stah • fkah zah…
day	**dzień**
	dj'yehn'
hour	**godzinę**
	goh • dj'ee • neh
game	**mecz**
	mehch
round	**turę**
	too • reh
Can I rent [hire]…?	**Czy mogę wypożyczyć…?**
	chyh moh • geh vyh • poh • zhyh • chyhch'
golf clubs	**kije do golfa**
	kee • yeh doh gohl • fah
equipment	**sprzęt**
	spshehnt

| a racket | **rakietę** |
| | *rah • kyeh • teh* |

AT THE BEACH/POOL

Where's the beach/ pool?	**Gdzie jest plaża/basen?**
	gdj'yeh yehst plah • zhah/bah • sehn
Is there…?	**Czy jest…?**
	chyh yehst…
a kiddie pool	**brodzik**
	broh • dj'eek
an indoor/ outdoor pool	**basen kryty/odkryty**
	bah • sehn kryh • tyh/oht • kryh • tyh
a lifeguard	**ratownik**
	rah • tohv • n'eek
Is it safe to swim/ dive here?	**Można tu bezpiecznie pływać/skakać?**
	mohzh • nah too behs • pyehch • n'yeh pwyh • vach'/skah • kach'
Is it safe for children?	**Czy jest tu bezpiecznie dla dzieci?**
	chyh yehst too behs • pyehch • n'yeh dlah dj'eh • ch'ee
I'd like to rent [hire]…	**Chciałbym** *m***/Chciałabym** *f* **wypożyczyć…**
	hch'yahw • byhm /hch'yah • wah • byhm vyh • poh • zhyh • chyhch'…
a deck chair	**leżak**
	leh • zhahk
diving equipment	**sprzęt do nurkowania**
	spshehnt doh noor • koh • vah • n'yah
a jet-ski	**skuter wodny**
	skoo • tehr vohd • nyh
a motorboat	**motorówkę**
	moh • toh • roof • keh
a rowboat	**łódkę wiosłową**
	wood • keh vyohs • woh • vohm

snorkeling	**sprzęt do nurkowania z fajką**
	spshehnt doh
equipment	*noor•koh•vah•n'yah sfahy•kohm*
a surfboard	**deskę surfingową**
	dehs•keh soor•feen•goh•vohm
a towel	**ręcznik**
	rehn•chn'eek
an umbrella	**parasol**
	pah•rah•sohl
waterskis	**narty wodne**
	nahr•tyh vohd•neh
a windsurfer	**deskę windsurfingową**
	dehs•keh weend•soor•feen•goh•vohm
For…hours.	**Na…godzin.**
	nah…goh•dj'een

Poland's sandy Baltic coast beaches are very popular during the summer months. Swim only in places that are marked **plaża strzeżona** (supervised beach) and have a **ratownik** (lifeguard); be sure to obey safety notices. The Mazury Lake District in the north-eastern part of Poland and the Greater Poland Lake District in the north-west are popular tourist destinations, especially for water sports lovers (swimming, sailing, windsurfing, fishing, diving and canoeing).

WINTER SPORTS

| A lift pass for a day/ five days, please. | **Poproszę jednodniowy/pięciodniowy skipass.** |
| | *poh•proh•sheh yehd•noh•dn'yoh•vyh/ pyehn'•ch'yoh•dn'yoh•vyh skee•pahs* |

I'd like to rent [hire]…	**Chciałbym** m/**Chciałabym** f **wypożyczyć…**
	hch'yahw • byhm/_hch'yah_ • wah • byhm fvyh • poh • _zhyh_ • chyhch'…
boots	**buty narciarskie**
	boo • tyh nahr • _ch'yahr_ • skyeh
cross-country skis	**biegówki**
	byeh • _goof_ • kee
a helmet	**kask**
	kahsk
poles	**kijki**
	keey • kee
skates	**łyżwy**
	wyhzh • vyh
skis	**narty**
	nahr • tyh
a snowboard	**deskę snowboardową**
	dehs • keh snowh • bohr • _doh_ • vohm
snowshoes	**rakiety śnieżne**
	rah • _kyeh_ • tyh sh'n'yehzh • neh
These are too big/ small.	**Te są za duże/małe.**
	teh sohm zah _doo_ • zheh/_mah_ • weh
Are there ski/ snowboard lessons?	**Czy jest nauka jazdy na nartach/ snowboardzie?**
	chyh yehst nah • _oo_ • kah _yahz_ • dyh nah _nahr_ • tahh/snowh • _bohr_ • dj'yeh
I'm a beginner.	**Jestem początkujący** m/**początkująca** f.
	yehs • tehm poh • chohn • tkoo • _yohn_ • tsyh/ poh • chohn • tkoo • _yohn_ • tsah
I'm experienced.	**Jestem zaawansowany** m/ **zaawansowana** f.
	yehs • tehm zah • ah • vahn • soh • _vah_ • nyh/ zah • ah • vahn • soh • _vah_ • nah

A trail [piste] map, please.	**Poproszę mapę tras.**
	poh • proh • sheh mah • peh trahs

There are many ski resorts in southern Poland, the most popular being **Zakopane**, **Szczyrk** and **Wisła**. The high **Tatra Mountains** offer excellent downhill skiing, and there are plenty of skiing opportunities on the lower slopes of many other mountains.

YOU MAY SEE...

WYCIĄG	drag lift
KOLEJKA LINOWA/GONDOLA	cable car/ gondola
WYCIĄG KRZESEŁKOWY	chair lift
TRASA ŁATWA	novice
TRASA TRUDNA	intermediate
TRASA BARDZO TRUDNA	expert
TRASA ZAMKNIĘTA	trail [piste] closed
UWAGA LAWINY	caution, avalanches

OUT IN THE COUNTRY

I'd like a map of...	**Poproszę mapę...**
	poh • proh • sheh mah • peh...
this region	**tego regionu**
	teh • goh reh • gyoh • noo
the walking routes	**tras pieszych**
	trahs pieh • shyhh

the bike routes	**szlaków rowerowych**
	shlah • koof roh • veh • roh • vyhh
the trails	**szlaków**
	shlah • koof
Is it far?	**Czy to daleko?**
	chyh toh dah • leh • koh
Is it easy/difficult?	**Czy to łatwa/trudna trasa?**
	chyh toh wah • tvah/troo • dnah trah • sah
Is it steep?	**Jest stromo?**
	yehst stroh • moh
How far is it to…?	**Jak daleko jest do…?**
	yahk dah • leh • koh yehst doh
I'm lost.	**Zgubiłem _m_/Zgubiłam _f_ się.**
	zgoo • bee • wehm/zgoo • bee • wahm
	sh'yeh
Where's…?	**Gdzie jest…?**
	gdj'yeh yehst…
the bridge	**most**
	mohst
the cave	**jaskinia**
	yahs • kee • n'yah
the cliff	**klif**
	kleef
the farm	**gospodarstwo**
	goh • spoh • dahr • stvoh
the field	**pole**
	poh • leh
the forest	**las**
	lahs
the lake	**jezioro**
	yeh • zh'yoh • roh
the mountain	**góra**
	goo • rah
the national park	**park narodowy**
	pahrk nah • roh • doh • vyh

the nature reserve	**rezerwat przyrody**
	reh • zehr • vaht pshyh • roh • dyh
the overlook	**punkt widokowy**
[viewpoint]	*poonkt vee • doh • koh • vyh*
the park	**park**
	pahrk
the path	**ścieżka**
	sh'ch'yesh • kah
the peak	**szczyt**
	sh • chyht
the picnic area	**pole piknikowe**
	poh • leh peek • n'ee • koh • veh
the pond	**staw**
	stahv
the river	**rzeka**
	zheh • kah
the sea	**morze**
	moh • zheh
the (thermal)	**(gorące) źródło**
spring	*(goh • rohn • tseh) zh'rood • woh*
the stream	**strumień**
	stroo • myehn'
the valley	**dolina**
	doh • lee • nah
the vineyard	**winnica**
	veen • nee • tsah
the waterfall	**wodospad**
	voh • dohs • paht

For Asking Directions, see page 64.

TRAVELING WITH CHILDREN

NEED TO KNOW

Is there a discount for children?	**Czy jest zniżka dla dzieci?** *chyh yehst <u>zn'eezh</u> • kah dlah <u>dj'yeh</u> • ch'ee*
Can you recommend a babysitter?	**Czy może pan polecić opiekunkę do dzieci?** *chyh <u>moh</u> • zheh pahn poh • <u>leh</u> • ch'eech' oh • pyeh • <u>koon</u> • keh doh <u>dj'yeh</u> • ch'ee*
Do you have a child's seat/highchair?	**Mają państwo krzesełko dla dziecka/wysokie krzesełko?** *<u>mah</u> • yohm <u>pahn</u> • stfoh ksheh • <u>seh</u> • wkoh dlah <u>dj'yeh</u> • tskah/ vyh • <u>soh</u> • kyeh ksheh • <u>seh</u> • wkoh*
Where can I change the baby?	**Gdzie mogę przewinąć dziecko?** *gdj'yeh <u>moh</u> • geh psheh • <u>vee</u> • nohn'ch' <u>dj'yehts</u> • koh*

OUT & ABOUT

Can you recommend something for kids?	**Czy może pan polecić coś dla dzieci?** *chyh <u>moh</u> • zheh pahn poh • <u>leh</u> • ch'eech' tsohsh' dlah <u>dj'yeh</u> • ch'ee*
Where's…?	**Gdzie jest…?** *gdj'yeh yehst…*
the amusement park	**wesołe miasteczko** *veh • <u>soh</u> • weh myahs • <u>teh</u> • chkoh*
the arcade	**salon gier** *<u>sah</u> • lohn gyehr*
the kiddie [paddling] pool	**brodzik** *<u>broh</u> • dj'eek*
the park	**park** *pahrk*
the playground	**plac zabaw** *plahts <u>zah</u> • bahf*
the zoo	**zoo** *<u>zoh</u> • oh*
Are children allowed?	**Czy można wchodzić z dziećmi?** *chyh <u>mohzh</u> • nah <u>fhoh</u> • dj'eech' zdj'yehch' • mee*
Is it safe for kids?	**Czy to jest bezpieczne dla dzieci?** *chyh toh yehst behs • <u>pyehch</u> • neh dlah <u>dj'yeh</u> • ch'ee*
Is it suitable for… year olds?	**Czy to jest odpowiednie dla…-latków?** *chyh toh yehst oht • poh • <u>vyehd</u> • n'yeh dlah…-<u>laht</u> • koof*

For Numbers, see page 20.

YOU MAY HEAR...

Jakie słodkie!	How cute!
yah • kyeh <u>swoht</u> • kyeh	
Jak ma na imię?	What's his/her
yahk mah nah <u>ee</u> • myeh	name?
Ile ma lat?	How old is he/
<u>ee</u> • leh mah laht	she?

BABY ESSENTIALS

Do you have...?	**Czy mają państwo...?** *chyh <u>mah</u> • yohm <u>pahn</u>' • stfoh...*
a baby bottle	**butelkę ze smoczkiem**
	boo • <u>tehl</u> • keh zeh <u>smohch</u> • kyehm
baby wipes	**wilgotne chusteczki pielęgnacyjne**
	veel • <u>goht</u> • neh hoos • <u>tehch</u> • kee pyeh • lehn • gnah • <u>tsyhy</u> • neh
a car seat	**fotelik samochodowy**
	foh • <u>teh</u> • leek sah • moh • hoh • <u>doh</u> • vyh
a child's seat/ highchair	**krzesełko dla dziecka/wysokie krzesełko**
	ksheh • <u>seh</u> • wkoh dlah <u>dj'yeh</u> • tskah/ vyh • <u>soh</u> • kyeh ksheh • <u>seh</u> • wkoh
a crib/cot	**łóżko składane/łóżeczko dziecięce**
	woo • shkoh skwah • <u>dah</u> • neh/ woo • <u>zhehch</u> • koh dj'yeh • <u>ch'ehn</u> • tseh
diapers [nappies]	**pieluszki**
	pyeh • <u>loosh</u> • kee
a pacifier [dummy]	**smoczek**
	smoh • chehk
a playpen	**kojec**
	<u>koh</u> • yehts

a stroller [pushchair]	**wózek spacerowy**
	voo•zehk spah•tseh•roh•vyh
Can I breastfeed the baby here?	**Czy mogę tutaj karmić dziecko piersią?**
	chyh moh•geh too•tay kahr•meech' dj'yehts koh pyehr•sh'yohm
Where can I change the baby?	**Gdzie mogę przewinąć dziecko?**
	gdj'yeh moh•geh psheh•vee•nohn'ch' dj'yehts•koh

For Dining with Children, see page 168.

BABYSITTING

Can you recommend a babysitter?	**Czy może pan polecić opiekunkę do dzieci?**
	chyh moh•zheh pahn poh•leh•ch'eech' oh•pyeh•koon•keh doh dj'yeh•ch'ee
What's the charge?	**Jaka jest opłata?**
	yah•kah yehst oh•pwah•tah
I'll be back by…	**Przyjdę za…**
	pshyhy•deh zah…
I can be reached at…	**Można do mnie dzwonić na numer…**
	moh•zhnah doh mn'yeh dzvoh•n'eech' nah noo•mehr…

SAFE TRAVEL

NEED TO KNOW

Help!	**Pomocy!**
	poh • moh • tsyh
Go away!	**Proszę odejść!**
	proh • sheh oh • deysh'ch'
Leave me alone!	**Zostaw mnie w spokoju!**
	zoh • stahf mn'yeh fspoh • koh • yoo
Stop thief!	**Łapać złodzieja!**
	wah • pach' zwoh • dj'yeh • yah
Get a doctor!	**Wezwijcie lekarza!**
	vez • veey • ch'yeh leh • kah • zhah
Fire!	**Pali się!**
	pah • lee sh'yeh
I'm lost.	**Zgubiłem się** *m/***Zgubiłam się** *f.*
	zgoo • bee • wehm sh'yeh/
	zgoo • bee • wahm sh'yeh
Can you help me?	**Czy może mi pan pomóc?**
	chyh moh • zheh mee pahn poh • moots

YOU MAY HEAR...

Proszę wypełnić ten formularz.
proh • sheh vyh • _pehw_ • n'eech' tehn
fohr • _moo_ • lash'

Please fill out
this form.

Poproszę dowód tożsamości.
poh • _proh_ • sheh _doh_ • voot
tohsh' • sah • _mohsh_' • ch'ee

Your
identification,
please.

Gdzie/Kiedy to się stało?
gdj'eh/_kyeh_ • dyh toh sh'yeh _stah_ • woh

When/Where did
it happen?

Jak on/ona wygląda?
yahk ohn/_oh_ • nah vyh • _glohn_ • dah

What does he/
she look like?

Proszę tu poczekać.
proh • sheh too poh • _cheh_ • kahch'

Please wait here.

Jak można się z panem skontaktować?
yahk _moh_ • zhnah sh'yeh spah • nehm
skohn • tahk • _toh_ • vahch'

How may we
contact you?

In an emergency, dial: **112** for the police
998 for the fire brigade
999 for the ambulance

POLICE

NEED TO KNOW

Call the police!	**Wezwijcie policję!** *vez • veey • ch'yeh poh • leets • yeh*
Where's the police station?	**Gdzie jest komisariat?** *gdj'yeh yehst koh • mee • sahr • yaht*
There has been an accident/attack.	**Zdarzył się wypadek/napad.** *zdah • zhyhw sh'yeh vyh • pah • dehk/ nah • paht*
My child is missing.	**Moje dziecko się zgubiło.** *moh • yeh dj'yeh • tskoh sh'yeh zgoo • bee • woh*
I need...	**Potrzebuję...** *poh • tsh'eh • boo • yeh...*
an interpreter	**tłumacza** *twoo • mah • chah*
to contact my lawyer	**skontaktować się z moim prawnikiem** *skohn • tah • ktoh • vahch' sh'yeh zmoh • eem prah • vn'ee • kyehm*
to make a phone call	**zatelefonować** *zah • teh • leh • foh • noh • vach'*
I'm innocent.	**Jestem niewinny** *m/***niewinna** *f.* *yeh • stehm n'yeh • veen • nyh/ n'yeh • veen • nah*
It was an accident.	**To był wypadek.** *toh byhw vyh • pah • dehk*

CRIME & LOST PROPERTY

I want to report…	**Chcę zgłosić…**
	htseh <u>zgwoh</u> • sh'eech'…
a mugging	**napad**
	<u>nah</u> • paht
a rape	**gwałt**
	gvahwt
a theft	**kradzież**
	<u>krah</u> • djyesh
I've been robbed/	**Okradli/Napadli mnie.**
mugged.	*oh • <u>krah</u> • dlee/nah • <u>pah</u> • dlee mn'yeh*
I've lost my…	**Zgubiłem…** *m*/**Zgubiłam…** *f*
	zgoo • <u>bee</u> • wehm…/zgoo • <u>bee</u> • wahm…
My…has been stolen.	**Ukradli mi…**
	oo • <u>krah</u> • dlee mee…
luggage	**bagaż**
	<u>bah</u> • gahsh
backpack	**plecak**
[rucksack]	*<u>pleh</u> • tsahk*
bicycle	**rower**
	roh • vehr
camera	**aparat fotograficzny**
	ah • <u>pah</u> • raht foh • toh • grah • <u>feech</u> • nyh

video camera	**kamerę**
	kah • meh • reh
(rental [hire]) car	**(wynajęty) samochód**
	(vyh • nah • yen • tyh) sah • moh • hoot
laptop	**laptop**
	lahp • tohp
credit card	**kartę kredytową**
	kahr • teh kreh • dyh • toh • vohm
cell [mobile] phone	**komórkę**
	koh • moor • keh
jewelry	**biżuterię**
	bee • zhoo • tehr • yeh
money	**pieniądze**
	pyeh • n'yohn • dzeh
passport	**paszport**
	pahsh • pohrt
purse [handbag]	**torebkę**
	toh • rehp • keh
travelers checks	**czeki podróżne**
	cheh • kee pohd • roozh • neh
wallet	**portfel**
	pohrt • fehl
I need a police report.	**Muszę mieć raport z policji.**
	moo • sheh myehch' rah • pohrt spoh • leets • yee
Where is the British/ American/Irish embassy?	**Gdzie jest ambasada brytyjska/ amerykańska/ irlandzka?**
	gdj'yeh yehst ahm • bah • sah • dah bryh • tyhy • skah/ ah • meh • ryh • kahn' • skah/ eer • lahntskah

HEALTH

NEED TO KNOW

I'm sick [ill].	**Jestem chory** m/**chora** f.
	yeh • stehm hoh • ryh /hoh • rah
I don't feel well.	**Źle się czuję.**
	zh'leh sh'yeh choo • yeh
Is there an English-speaking doctor?	**Czy jest tu lekarz mówiący po angielsku?**
	chyh yehst too leh • kahsh moo • vyohn • tsyh poh ahn • gyehls • koo
It hurts here.	**Boli mnie tutaj.**
	boh • lee mn'yeh too • tay
I have a stomachache.	**Boli mnie brzuch.**
	boh • lee mn'yeh bzhooh

FINDING A DOCTOR

Can you recommend a doctor/dentist?	**Czy może pan polecić lekarza/ dentystę?**
	chyh moh • zheh pahn poh • leh • ch'eech' leh • kah • zhah/dehn • tyh • steh
Could the doctor come to see me here?	**Czy lekarz może przyjść mnie zbadać tutaj?**
	chyh leh • kash moh • zheh pshyhysh'ch' mn'yeh zbah • dach' too • tay
I need an English-speaking doctor.	**Potrzebuję lekarza mówiącego po angielsku.**
	poht • sheh • boo • yeh leh • kah • zhah moo • vyohn • tseh • goh poh ahn • gyehls • koo

What are the office [surgery] hours?	**Jakie są godziny przyjęć?**
	yahk • yeh sohm goh • dj'ee • nyh pshyh • yehnch'
Can I make an appointment…?	**Czy mogę zamówić wizytę…?**
	chyh moh • geh zah • moo • veech' vee • zyh • teh…
for today	**na dzisiaj**
	nah dj'ee • sh'yahy
for tomorrow	**na jutro**
	nah yoo • troh
as soon as possible	**na jak najbliższy termin**
	nah yahk nahy • bleesh • shyh tehr • meen
It's urgent.	**To jest pilne.**
	toh yest peel • neh
It's an emergency.	**To nagły wypadek.**
	toh nah • gwyh vyh • pah • dehk

SYMPTOMS

I'm…	**Mam…**
	mahm…
bleeding	**krwotok**
	krfoh • tohk
constipated	**zaparcie**
	zah • pahr • ch'yeh
dizzy	**zawroty głowy**
	zah • vroh • tyh gwoh • vyh
nauseous	**mdłości**
	mdwosh' • ch'ee
I'm vomiting.	**Wymiotuję.**
	vyh • myoh • too • yeh
It hurts here.	**Boli mnie tutaj.**
	boh • lee mn'yeh too • tay
I have…	**Mam…**
	mahm…

an allergic reaction	**reakcję alergiczną**
	reh • ahk • tsyeh ah • lehr • geech • nohm
chest pain	**bóle w klatce piersiowej**
	boo • leh f klaht • tseh pyehr • sh'yoh • vey
a fever	**gorączkę**
	goh • rohnch • keh
pain	**bóle**
	boo • leh
a rash	**wysypkę**
	vyh • syhp • keh
a sprain	**zwichnięcie**
	zvee • hn'yehn' • ch'yeh
some swelling	**opuchliznę**
	oh • poo • hleez • neh
sunstroke	**udar słoneczny**
	oo • dahr swoh • nehch • nyh
I have…	**Boli mnie…**
	boh • lee mn'yeh…
an earache	**ucho**
	oo • hoh
a stomachache	**brzuch**
	bzhooh
a headache	**głowa**
	gwoh • vah
I've been sick for… days.	**Źle się czuję od…dni.**
	zh'leh sh'yeh choo • yeh oht…dn'yee

For Numbers, see page 20.

YOU MAY HEAR...

W czym problem?
fchyhm proh • blehm

What's wrong?

Gdzie boli?
gdj'yeh boh • lee

Where does it hurt?

Czy boli tutaj?
chyh boh • lee too • tay

Does it hurt here?

Czy przyjmuje pan regularnie leki?
chyh pshyhy • moo • yeh pahn reh • goo • lahr • n'yeh leh • kee

Are you on medication?

Czy jest pan na coś uczulony?
chyh yehst pahn nah tsosh' oo • choo • loh • nyh

Are you allergic to anything?

Proszę otworzyć usta.
proh • sheh oht • foh • zhyhch' oo • stah

Please open your mouth.

Oddychać głęboko.
ohd • dyh • hach' gwehm • boh • koh

Breathe deeply.

Pójdzie pan do szpitala.
pooy • dj'yeh pahn doh shpee • tah • lah

You must go to the hospital.

CONDITIONS

I'm…	**Mam…**
	mahm…
anemic	**anemię**
	ah • neh • myeh
asthmatic	**astmę**
	ahst • meh
diabetic	**cukrzycę**
	tsook • shyh • tseh
epileptic	**Mam padaczkę**
	mahm pah • dah • chkeh
I'm allergic to antibiotics/ penicillin.	**Mam uczulenie na antybiotyki/ penicylinę.**
	Mahm oo • choo • leh • n'yeh
	nah ahn • tyh • byoh • tyh • kee/ peh • nee • tsyh • lee • neh
I have arthritis.	**Mam artretyzm.**
	mahm ahr • treh • tyhsm
I have high/low blood pressure.	**Mam wysokie/niskie ciśnienie.**
	mahm vyh • soh • kyeh/nees • kyeh ch'eesh' • n'yeh • n'yeh
I have a heart condition.	**Choruję na serce.**
	hoh • roo • yeh na sehr • tseh
I'm on…	**Zażywam…**
	zah • zhyh • vahm…

For Dietary Requirements, see page 167.

TREATMENT

Do I need a prescription/ medicine?	**Czy potrzebuję lekarstwa/recepty?**
	chyh poh • tzheh • boo • yeh leh • kahrs • tfah/ reh • tsehp • tyh

Can you prescribe a generic drug [unbranded medication]?	**Czy mogę prosić o przepisanie leku generycznego [niemarkowego]?**
	chyh <u>moh</u> • geh proh • sh'eech' oh psh'eh • pee • <u>sah</u> • nyeh <u>leh</u> • koo geh • neh • ryhch • <u>neh</u> • goh (n'ye • mahr • koh • <u>veh</u> • goh)
Where can I get it?	**Gdzie to mogę dostać?**
	Gdj'yeh toh <u>moh</u> • geh doh • stahch'

For Pharmacy, see page 151.

HOSPITAL

Please notify my family.	**Proszę zawiadomić moją rodzinę.**
	<u>proh</u> • sheh zah • vyah • <u>doh</u> • meech' <u>moh</u> • yohm roh • <u>dj'ee</u> • neh
I'm in pain.	**Boli mnie.**
	<u>boh</u> • lee mn'yeh
I need a doctor/ nurse.	**Potrzebuję lekarza/pielęgniarki.**
	poh • tsheh • <u>boo</u> • yeh leh • <u>kah</u> • zhah/ pyeh • lehng • <u>n'yahr</u> • kee
When are visiting hours?	**Jakie są godziny odwiedzin?**
	<u>yah</u> • kyeh sohm goh • <u>dj'ee</u> • nyh ohd • <u>vyeh</u> • dj'een
I'm visiting…	**Odwiedzam…**
	ohd • <u>vyeh</u> • dzahm…

YOU MAY HEAR…

Musimy zrobić rentgen.	We must X-ray you.
moo • <u>sh'ee</u> • myh zroh • beech' rehnt • gehn	
Proszę podpisać zgodę na operację.	Please sign the consent for surgery.
<u>proh</u> • sheh poht • pee • sahch' <u>zgoh</u> • deh nah oh • peh • <u>rah</u> • tsyeh	

DENTIST

I've lost a filling.	**Wypadła mi plomba.**
	vyh • _pahd_ • wah mee _plohm_ • bah
I've lost a tooth.	**Wypadł mi ząb.**
	vyh • pahdw mee zohmp
I have a toothache.	**Boli mnie ząb.**
	boh • lee mn'yeh zohmp
Can you fix this denture?	**Czy da się naprawić tę protezę?**
	chyh dah sh'yeh nah • _prah_ • veech' teh
	proh • _teh_ • zeh
I'd like an anesthetic.	**Poproszę znieczulenie.**
	poh • _proh_ • sheh zn'yeh • choo • _leh_ • n'yeh

GYNECOLOGIST

I have menstrual cramps/a vaginal infection.	**Mam bóle miesiączkowe/infekcję pochwy.**
	mahm _boo_ • leh
	myeh • sh'yohn • chkoh • veh/
	een • _fehk_ • tsyeh poh • hfyh
I missed my period.	**Spóźnia mi się okres.**
	spoo • zh'n'yah mee sh'yeh _ohk_ • rehs
I'm on the pill.	**Biorę pigułki antykoncepcyjne.**
	byoh • reh pee • _goow_ • kee
	ahn • tyh • kohn • tsep • _tsyhy_ • neh
I'm (not) pregnant.	**(Nie) Jestem w ciąży.**
	(n'yeh) _yehs_ • tehm _fch'yohn_ • zhyh
I haven't had my period for...months.	**Nie miałam okresu od...miesięcy.**
	n'yeh _myah_ • wahm oh • _kreh_ • soo oht...
	myeh • _sh'yen_ • tsyh

For Numbers, see page 20.

OPTICIAN

I've lost…	**Zgubiłem** *m*/**Zgubiłam** *f* …
	zgoo • bee • wehm/zgoo • bee • wahm …
a contact lens	**soczewkę kontaktową**
	soh • chehf • keh kohn • tahk • toh • vohm
my glasses	**okulary**
	oh • koo • lah • ryh
a lens	**soczewkę**
	soh • chef • keh

PAYMENT & INSURANCE

How much?	**Ile to kosztuje?**
	ee • leh toh kohsh • too • yeh
Can I pay by credit card?	**Czy mogę zapłacić kartą kredytową?**
	chyh moh • geh zah • pwah • ch'eech' kahr • tohm kreh • dyh • toh • vohm
I have insurance.	**Mam ubezpieczenie.**
	mam oo • behs • pyeh • che • n'yeh
Can I have a receipt for my insurance?	**Czy mogę dostać pokwitowanie dla mojego ubezpieczenia?**
	chyh moh • geh dohs • tach' poh • kfee • toh • vah • n'yeh dlah moh • yeh • goh oo • behs • pyeh • cheh • n'yah

For Money, see page 31.

PHARMACY

NEED TO KNOW

Where's the nearest (24-hour) pharmacy?	**Gdzie jest najbliższa apteka (całodobowa)?**
	gdj'yeh yest nay • bleesh • sha ah • pteh • kah
	(tsah • woh • doh • boh • vah)
What time does the pharmacy open/ close?	**O której otwierają/zamykają aptekę?**
	oh ktoo • rey oht • fyeh • rah • yohm/ zah • myh • kah • yohm ah • pteh • keh
What would you recommend for...?	**Co może mi pan polecić na...?**
	tsoh moh • zheh mee pahn poh • leh • ch'eech' nah...
How much do I take?	**Ile mam brać?**
	ee • leh mahm brahch'
Can you fill this prescription?	**Czy możecie zrealizować tę receptę?**
	chyh moh • zheh • ch'yeh zreh • ah • lee • zoh • vach' teh reh • tsehp • teh
I'm allergic to...	**Mam uczulenie na...**
	mahm oo • choo • leh • n'yeh nah...

WHAT TO TAKE

I'd like some medicine for...	**Poproszę lekarstwo na...**
	poh • proh • sheh leh • kahrs • tfoh nah...
a cold	**przeziębienie**
	psheh • zh'yehm • byeh • n'yeh

Pharmacies in Poland are easily identifiable by the sign **APTEKA** and a cross. Opening hours are generally from 9:00 a.m. to 6:00 p.m.; some operate around the clock. The names and locations of these 24-hour pharmacies are posted on the doors and windows of other pharmacies. You will need a prescription for drugs not available over the counter. Most pharmacies nowadays sell toiletries and cosmetics, too.

a cough	**kaszel**
	kah • shehl
a headache	**ból głowy**
	boohl gwoh • vyh
diarrhea	**biegunkę**
	byeh • goon • keh
the flu	**grypę**
	gryh • peh
motion [travel] sickness	**chorobę lokomocyjną**
	hoh • roh • beh
	loh • koh • moh • tsyhy • nohm
a sore throat	**ból gardła**
	bool gahr • dwah
a toothache	**ból zęba**
	boohl zehm • bah
an upset stomach	**rozstrój żołądka**
	rohs • strooy zhoh • wohnt • kah
How much should I take?	**Ile mam wziąć?**
	ee • leh mahm vzh'yonch'
How often should I take it?	**Jak często mam to brać?**
	yahk chehn • stoh mahm toh brahch'
Is it suitable for children?	**Czy to jest odpowiednie dla dzieci?**
	chyh toh yest oht • poh • vyehd • n'yeh dlah dj'yeh • ch'ee

I'm on…	**Biorę…**
	byoh • reh…
Are there side effects?	**Czy są jakieś efekty uboczne?**
	chyh sohm <u>yah</u> • kyesh' eh • <u>fehk</u> • tyh oo • <u>bohch</u> • neh

---

YOU MAY HEAR...

RAZ/TRZY RAZY DZIENNIE	once/three times a day
TABLETKA	tablet
KROPLA	drop
ŁYŻECZKA	teaspoon
PRZED POSIŁKIEM	before meals
PO/W TRAKCIE POSIŁKU	after/with meals
NA CZCZO	on an empty stomach
POŁYKAĆ W CAŁOŚCI	swallow whole
MOŻE POWODOWAĆ SENNOŚĆ	may cause drowsiness
WYŁĄCZNIE DO UŻYTKU ZEWNĘTRZNEGO	for external use only

BASIC SUPPLIES

I'd like…	**Poproszę…**
	poh • <u>proh</u> • sheh…
acetaminophen [paracetamol]	**paracetamol**
	pah • rah • tseh • <u>tah</u> • mohl
antiseptic cream	**krem aseptyczny**
	krehm ah • sehp • <u>tyhch</u> • nyh
aspirin	**aspirynę**
	ah • spee • <u>ryh</u> • neh

a bandage	**bandaż**
	bahn • dahzh
a comb	**grzebień**
	gzheh • byen'
condoms	**prezerwatywy**
	preh • zehr • vah • _tyh_ • vyh
contact lens solution	**płyn do soczewek kontaktowych**
	pwyhn doh soh • _cheh_ • vehk kohn • tahk • _toh_ • vyh
deodorant	**dezodorant**
	deh • zoh • _doh_ • rahnt
a hairbrush	**szczotkę do włosów**
	shchoht • keh doh _vwoh_ • soof
hair spray	**lakier do włosów**
	lah • kyehr doh _vwoh_ • soof
ibuprofen	**ibuprofen**
	ee • boo • _proh_ • fehn
insect repellent	**środek na owady**
	sh'roh • dehk nah oh • _vah_ • dyh
lotion	**balsam**
	bahl • sahm
a nail file	**pilnik do paznokci**
	peel • n'eek doh pahz • _nohk_ • ch'ee
painkillers	**środki przeciwbólowe**
	sh'roht • kee psheh • ch'eef • boo • _loh_ • veh
a (disposable) razor	**(jednorazową) maszynkę do golenia**
	(yehd • noh • rah • _zoh_ • vohm) mah • _shyhn_ • keh doh goh • _leh_ • n'yah
razor blades	**żyletki**
	zhyh • _leht_ • kee
sanitary napkins [towels]	**podpaski**
	poht • _pahs_ • kee
shampoo/ conditioner	**szampon/odżywkę**
	shahm • pohn/ohd • _zhyhf_ • keh

soap	**mydło**
	myh • dwoh
sunscreen	**krem do opalania**
	krehm doh oh • pah • _lah_ • n'yah
tampons	**tampony**
	tahm • _poh_ • nyh
tissues	**chusteczki papierowe**
	hoos • _tech_ • kee pahp • yeh • _roh_ • veh
toilet paper	**papier toaletowy**
	pah • pyehr toh • ah • leh • _toh_ • vyh
a toothbrush	**szczoteczkę do zębów**
	shchoh • _tech_ • keh doh _zehm_ • boof
toothpaste	**pastę do zębów**
	pah • steh doh _zehm_ • boof

For Baby Essentials, see page 134.

CHILD HEALTH & EMERGENCY

Can you recommend a pediatrician?	**Czy może pan polecić pediatrę?**
	chyh _moh_ • zheh pahn poh • _leh_ • ch'eech' peh • _dyaht_ • reh
My child is allergic to…	**Moje dziecko ma uczulenie na…**
	moh • yeh dj'yeh • tskoh mah oo • choo • _leh_ • n'yeh nah…
My child is missing.	**Moje dziecko się zgubiło.**
	moh • yeh dj'yeh • tskoh sh'yeh zgoo • _bee_ • woh
Have you seen a boy/girl?	**Czy widział pan chłopca/dziewczynkę?**
	chyh _vee_ • dj'yahw pahn _hwohp_ • tsah/dj'yehv • _chyhn_ • keh

For Police, see page 140.

DISABLED TRAVELERS

NEED TO KNOW

Is there…?	**Czy jest…?** *chyh yehst…*
access for the disabled	**dostęp dla niepełnosprawnych** *dohs • tehmp dlah* *n'yeh • pehw • noh • sprahv • nyhh*
a wheelchair ramp	**podjazd dla wózków inwalidzkich** *pohd • yahst dlah voos • koof* *een • vah • leets • keeh*
a disabled-accessible toilet	**toaleta dla niepełnosprawnych** *toh • ah • leh • tah dlah* *n'yeh • pew • noh • sprahv • nyhh*
I need…	**Potrzebuję…** *poh • tsheh • boo • yeh…*
assistance	**pomocy** *poh • moh • tsyh*
an elevator [lift]	**windy** *veen • dyh*
a ground-floor room	**pokoju na parterze** *poh • koh • yoo nah pahr • teh • zheh*

ASKING FOR ASSISTANCE

I'm disabled.	**Jestem nepełnosprawny** *m/* **niepełnosprawna** *f.* *yehs • tehm* *n'yeh • pehw • noh • sprahv • nyh/* *n'yeh • pehw • noh • sprahv • nah*

I'm deaf.	**Jestem głuchy** *m*/**głucha** *f*.
	yehs • tehm gwoo • hyh/gwoo • hah
I'm visually/hearing impaired.	**Niedowidzę./Niedosłyszę.**
	n'yeh • doh • vee • dzeh/
	n'yeh • doh • swyh • sheh
I'm unable to walk far/use the stairs.	**Nie mogę dużo chodzić/chodzić po schodach.**
	n'yeh moh • geh doo • zhoh hoh • dj'eech'/
	hoh • dj'eech' poh s • hoh • dahh
Can I bring my wheelchair?	**Czy mogę być na wózku inwalidzkim?**
	chyh moh • geh byhch' nah voos • koo
	een • vah • leets • keem
Are guide dogs permitted?	**Czy mogę być z psem przewodnikiem?**
	chyh moh • geh byhch' spsehm
	psheh • vohd • n'ee • kyem
Can you help me?	**Czy może mi pan pomóc?**
	chyh moh • zheh mee pahn poh • moots
Please open/hold the door.	**Proszę otworzyć/przytrzymać drzwi.**
	proh • sheh oht • foh • zhyhch'/
	pshyh • tshyh • mahch' djvee

For Emergencies, see page 138.

FOOD

EATING OUT

NEED TO KNOW

Can you recommend a good restaurant/cafe?	**Czy może mi pan polecić dobrą restaurację/kawiarnię?** *chyh moh • zheh mee pahn poh • leh • ch'eech' dohb • rohm rehs • tahw • rahts • yeh/ kah • vyahr • n'yeh*
Is there a traditional Polish/an inexpensive restaurant nearby?	**Czy jest tu gdzieś w pobliżu tradycyjna polska/niedroga restauracja?** *chyh yehst too gdj'yehsh' fpoh • blee • zhoo trah • dyh • tsyhy • nah pohls • kah/n'yeh • droh • gah rehs • tahw • rahts • yah*
A table for one/two, please.	**Stolik dla jednej osoby/dwóch osób, proszę.** *stoh • leek dlah yehd • nehy oh • soh • byh/dvooh oh • soop proh • sheh*
Can we sit...?	**Możemy usiąść...?** *moh • zheh • myh oo • sh'yohn'sh'ch'...*
here/there	**tu/tam** *too/tahm*
outside	**na zewnątrz** *nah zehv • nohntsh*
in a non-smoking area	**w części dla niepalących** *fchehn'sh' • ch'ee dlah n'yeh • pah • lohn • tsyhh*

Where are the toilets?	**Gdzie są toalety?**
	gdj'yeh sohm toh • ah • leh • tyh
Can I have a menu?	**Mogę prosić menu?**
	moh • geh proh • sh'eech' meh • n'ee
What do you recommend?	**Co może pan polecić?**
	tsoh moh • zheh pahn poh • leh • ch'eech'
I'd like…	**Poproszę…**
	poh • proh • sheh…
Some more…, please.	**Poproszę trochę więcej…**
	poh • proh • sheh troh • heh vyehn • tsehy…
Enjoy your meal.	**Smacznego.**
	smahch • neh • goh
The check [bill], please.	**Poproszę rachunek.**
	poh • proh • sheh rah • hoo • nehk
Is service included?	**Czy obsługa jest wliczona w cenę?**
	chyh ohp • swoo • gah yehst vlee • choh • nah ftseh • neh
Can I pay by credit card?	**Czy mogę zapłacić kartą kredytową?**
	chyh moh • geh zah • pwah • ch'eech' kahr • tohm kreh • dyh • toh • vohm
Can I have a receipt?	**Czy mogę prosić paragon?**
	chyh moh • geh pro • sh'eech' pah • rah • gohn
Thank you.	**Dziękuję.**
	dj'yehn • koo • yeh

WHERE TO EAT

Can you recommend…?	**Czy może pan polecić…?**
	chyh moh • zheh pahn poh • leh • ch'eech'…

a restaurant	**restaurację**
	rehs • tahw • <u>rahts</u> • yeh
a bar	**bar**
	bahr
a cafe	**kawiarnię**
	kah • <u>vyahr</u> • n'yeh
a fast-food place	**fast-food**
	<u>fahst</u> • foot
an ice-cream parlor	**lodziarnię**
	loh • <u>dj'yahr</u> • n'yeh
a pub	**pub**
	pahp
a cheap restaurant	**niedroga restauracja**
	n'yeh • <u>droh</u> • gah rehs • tahw • <u>rahts</u> • yah
an expensive restaurant	**droga restauracja**
	<u>droh</u> • gah rehs • tahw • <u>rahts</u> • yah
a restaurant with a good view	**restauracja z dobrym widokiem**
	rehs • tahw • <u>rahts</u> • yah zdohb • ryhm vee • <u>doh</u> • kyehm
an authentic/ a non-touristy restaurant	**tradycyjna restauracja/ restauracja lubiana przez miejscowych**
	trah • dyh • <u>tsyhy</u> • nah rehs • tahw • <u>rahts</u> • yah/ rehs • tahw • <u>rahts</u> • yah loo • <u>byah</u> • nah pshez myehys • <u>tsoh</u> • vyh

RESERVATIONS & PREFERENCES

I'd like to reserve a table…	**Chciałbym** *m*/**Chciałabym** *f* **zarezerwować stolik…**
	<u>hch'yahw</u> • byhm/<u>hch'yah</u> • wah • byhm zah • reh • zehr • <u>voh</u> • vahch' stoh • leek…
for two	**dla dwóch osób**
	dlah dvooh <u>oh</u> • soop

for this evening	**na dziś wieczór**
	nah dj'eesh' <u>vyeh</u> • choor
for tomorrow at…	**na jutro na…**
	nah <u>yoot</u> • roh nah…
A table for two, please.	**Proszę stolik dla dwóch osób.**
	proh • sheh <u>stoh</u> • leek dlah dvooh
	<u>oh</u> • soop
I have a reservation.	**Mam rezerwację.**
	mahm reh • zehr • <u>vahts</u> • yeh
My name is…	**Nazywam się…**
	nah • <u>zyh</u> • vahm sh'yeh…
Can we sit…?	**Możemy usiąść…?**
	moh • <u>zheh</u> • myh oo • sh'yohn'sh'ch'…
here/there	**tu/tam**
	too/tahm
outside	**na zewnątrz**
	nah <u>zehv</u> • nohntsh
in a non-smoking area	**w części dla niepalących**
	<u>fchehnsh'</u> • ch'ee dlah
	n'yeh • pah • <u>lohn</u> • tsyhh

YOU MAY HEAR…

Czy ma pan rezerwację?
chyh mah pahn reh • zehr • <u>vahts</u> • yeh
Do you have a reservation?

Dla ilu osób?
dlah <u>ee</u> • loo <u>oh</u> • soop
For how many?

Co podać?
tsoh poh • dahch'
What would you like?

Polecam…
poh • <u>leh</u> • tsahm…
I recommend…

Smacznego.
smahch • <u>neh</u> • goh
Enjoy your meal.

by the window	**przy oknie**
	pshyh <u>ohk</u> • n'yeh
in the shade	**w cieniu?**
	<u>fch'yeh</u> • n'yoo
in the sun	**w słońcu?**
	<u>fswhon'</u> • tsoo
Where are the toilets?	**Gdzie są toalety?**
	gdj'yeh sohm toh • ah • <u>leh</u> • tyh

HOW TO ORDER

Excuse me!	**Przepraszam!**
	psheh • <u>prah</u> • shahm
I'm ready to order.	**Chciałbym m/Chciałabym f już zamówić.**
	<u>hch'yahw</u> • byhm/<u>hch'yah</u> • wah • byhm yoosh zah • <u>moo</u> • veech'
May I see the wine list?	**Mogę prosić kartę win?**
	<u>moh</u> • geh <u>proh</u> • sheech' <u>kahr</u> • teh veen
I'd like…	**Poproszę…**
	poh • <u>proh</u> • sheh…
a bottle of…	**butelkę…**
	boo • <u>tehl</u> • keh…
a carafe of…	**karafkę…**
	kah • <u>rahf</u> • keh…
a glass of wine	**kieliszek wina**
	kyeh • <u>lee</u> • shehk vee • nah
a glass of water	**szklankę wody**
	<u>shklahn</u> • keh <u>voh</u> • dyh
Can I have a menu?	**Mogę prosić menu?**
	<u>moh</u> • geh <u>proh</u> • sh'eech' meh • <u>n'ee</u>
Do you have…?	**Czy mają państwo…?**
	chyh <u>mah</u> • yohm <u>pahn's</u> • tfoh…
a menu in English	**menu po angielsku**
	meh • <u>n'ee</u> poh ahn • <u>gyehls</u> • koo

a fixed-price menu	**zestawy**
	zehs • <u>tah</u> • vyh
a children's menu	**dania dla dzieci**
	<u>dah</u> • n'yah dlah <u>dj'yeh</u> • ch'ee
What do you recommend?	**Co może pan polecić?**
	tsoh moh • zheh pahn poh • <u>leh</u> • ch'eech'
What's this?	**Co to jest?**
	tso toh yehst
What's in it?	**Z czego to jest zrobione?**
	scheh • goh toh yehst zroh • <u>byoh</u> • neh
Is it spicy?	**Czy to jest ostre?**
	chyh toh yehst <u>oh</u> • streh
I'd like...	**Poproszę...**
	poh • <u>proh</u> • sheh...
More...please.	**Poproszę więcej...**
	poh • <u>proh</u> • sheh <u>vyehn</u> • tsehy...
With/Without... please.	**Poproszę z/bez...**
	poh • <u>proh</u> • sheh z/behs...
I can't eat...	**Nie mogę jeść...**
	n'yeh <u>moh</u> • geh yehsh'ch'...
rare	**krwisty**
	krfees • tyh
medium	**średnio wysmażony**
	sh'rehd • n'yoh vyhs • mah • <u>zhoh</u> • nyh
well-done	**dobrze wysmażony**
	<u>dohb</u> • zheh vyhs • mah • <u>zhoh</u> • nyh

It's to go [take away]. **Na wynos, poproszę.**

nah <u>vyh</u> • nohs poh • <u>proh</u> • sheh

For Drinks, see page 188.

COOKING METHODS

baked	**pieczony**
	pyeh • <u>choh</u> • nyh
boiled	**gotowany**
	goh • toh • <u>vah</u> • nyh
braised	**duszony**
	doo • <u>shoh</u> • nyh
breaded	**panierowany**
	pah • n'yeh • roh • <u>vah</u> • nyh
creamed	**starty**
	<u>stahr</u> • tyh
diced	**pokrojony w kostkę**
	poh • kroh • <u>yoh</u> • nyh <u>fkohs</u> • tkeh
filleted	**filet**
	<u>fee</u> • leht
fried	**smażony**
	smah • <u>zhoh</u> • nyh
grilled	**grillowany**
	gree • loh • <u>vah</u> • nyh
poached	**z wody**
	<u>zvoh</u> • dyh
roasted	**pieczony**
	pyeh • <u>choh</u> • nyh
sautéed	**smażony sauté**
	smah • <u>zhoh</u> • nyh soh • teh
smoked	**wędzony**
	vehn • <u>dzoh</u> • nyh
steamed	**gotowany na parze**
	goh • toh • <u>vah</u> • nyh nah <u>pah</u> • zheh

stewed	**duszony**
	doo • shoh • nyh
stuffed	**faszerowany**
	fah • sheh • roh • vah • nyh

DIETARY REQUIREMENTS

I'm…	**Jestem…**
	yehs • tehm…
allergic to…	**uczulony na…**
	oo • choo • loh • nyh nah…
diabetic	**cukrzykiem**
	yehs • tehm tsook • shyh • kyehm
lactose intolerant	**Mam nietolerancję laktozy**
	mahm n'yeh • toh • leh • rahn • tsyeh lahk • toh • zyh
vegetarian	**wegetarianinem** *m*/**wegetarianką** *f*
	veh • geh • tahr • yah • n'ee • nehm/ veg • geh • tah • ryahn • kohm
vegan	**weganinem** *m*/**weganką** *f*
	veh • gah • n'ee • nehm/veh • gahn • kohm
I can't eat…	**Nie mogę jeść…**
	n'yeh moh • geh yehsh'ch'…
dairy products	**produktów mlecznych**
	proh • dook • toof mlehch • nyhh
gluten	**glutenu**
	gloo • teh • noo
nuts	**orzechów**
	oh • zheh • hoof
pork	**wieprzowiny**
	vyehp • shoh • vee • nyh
shellfish	**owoców morza**
	oh • voh • tsoof moh • zhah
spicy food	**pikantnych potraw**
	pee • kahnt • nyhh poht • rahf

wheat	**pszenicy**
	psheh • n'ee • tsyh
Is it halal/kosher?	**Czy to jest halal/koszerne?**
	chyh toh yehst hah • lahl/koh • shehr • neh
Do you have…?	**Czy mają państwo…?**
	chyh mah • yohm pahn's • tfoh…
skimmed milk	**mleko odtłuszczone**
	mleh • koh ohd • twoosh • choh • neh
whole milk	**mleko pełne**
	mleh • koh pehw • neh
soya milk	**mleko sojowe**
	mleh • koh soh • yoh • veh

DINING WITH CHILDREN

Do you have children's portions?	**Mają państwo porcje dla dzieci?**
	mah • yohm pahn's • tfoh pohr • tsyeh dlah dj'yeh • ch'ee
Can I have a highchair/child's seat?	**Mógłbym m/Mogłabym f dostać wysokie krzesełko/krzesełko dla dziecka?**
	moogw • byhm/moh • gwah • byhm dohs • tahch' vyh • soh • kyeh ksheh • sehw • koh/ksheh • sehw • koh dlah dj'yehts • kah
Where can I feed/ change the baby?	**Gdzie mogę nakarmić/przewinąć dziecko?**
	gdj'yeh moh • geh nah • kahr • meech'/ psheh • vee • nohn'ch' dj'yehts • koh
Can you warm this?	**Może pan to podgrzać?**
	moh • zheh pahn toh pohd • gzhahch'

For Traveling with Children, see page 132.

HOW TO COMPLAIN

When will our food be ready?	**Jak długo jeszcze będziemy czekać na nasze zamówienie?**
	yahk dwoo • goh yehsh • cheh behn' • dj'yeh • myh cheh • kahch' nah nah • sheh zah • moo • vyeh • n'yeh
We can't wait any longer.	**Nie możemy dłużej czekać.**
	n'yeh moh • zheh • myh dwoo • zhehy cheh • kach'
We're leaving.	**Wychodzimy.**
	vyh • hoh • dj'ee • myh
I didn't order this.	**Nie zamawiałem** m/**zamawiałam** f **tego.**
	n'yeh zah • mah • vyah • wehm/ zah • mah • vyah • wahm teh • goh
I ordered…	**Zamawiałem** m/**Zamawiałam** f…
	zah • mah • vyah • wehm/ zah • mah • vyah • wahm…
I can't eat this.	**Nie mogę tego jeść.**
	n'yeh moh • geh teh • goh yehsh'ch'
This is too…	**To jest za…**
	toh yehst zah…
cold/hot	**zimne/gorące**
	zh'eem • neh/goh • rohn • tseh
salty/spicy	**słone/ostre**
	swoh • neh/ohs • treh
tough/bland	**twarde/mdłe**
	tfahr • deh/mdweh
This isn't fresh.	**To jest nieświeże.**
	toh yehst n'yeh • sh'fyeh • zheh
This is dirty.	**To jest brudne.**
	toh yehst brood • neh

PAYING

The check [bill], please.	**Poproszę rachunek.** *poh • proh • sheh rah • hoo • nehk*
Separate checks [bills], please.	**Chcielibyśmy zapłacić osobno.** *hch'yeh • lee • byhsh' • myh zah • pwah • ch'eech' oh • sohb • noh*
It's all together.	**Proszę policzyć wszystko razem.** *proh • sheh poh • lee • chyhch' fshyhst • koh rah • zehm*
Is service included?	**Czy obługa jest wliczona w cenę?** *chyh ohp • swoo • gah yehst vlee • choh • nah ftseh • neh*
What's this amount for?	**Za co jest ta kwota?** *zah tsoh yehst tah kfoh • tah*
I didn't have that.	**Nie jadłem m/ jadłam f tego** *n'yeh yahd • wehm/ yahd • wahm teh • goh*
I had…	**Zjadłem m/zjadłam f …** *zyahd • wehm/ zyahd • wahm …*
Can I pay by credit card?	**Można płacić kartą kredytową?** *mohzh • nah pwah • ch'eech' kahr • tohm kreh • deeh • toh • vohm*
Can I have an itemized bill/ a receipt?	**Czy mogę dostać szczegółowy rachunek/pokwitowanie?** *chyh moh • geh dohs • tahch' shcheh • goo • woh • vyh rah • hoo • nehk/ pohk • fee • toh • vah • n'yeh*
That was delicious.	**Bardzo mi smakowało.** *bahr • dzoh mee smah • koh • vah • woh*
I've already paid	**Już zapłaciłem m/zapłaciłam f.** *yoosh zah • pwah • ch'ee • wehm/ zah • pwah • ch'ee • wahm*

It is customary to tip your server 10% of the total bill.
In more expensive restaurants the head waiter should
also be tipped.

MEALS & COOKING

Traditional Polish cuisine was influenced by the
climate and location of Poland. Many dishes owe much
to neighboring Russia, Germany and Hungary. Heavy
soup, meat with root and/or pickled vegetables, cabbage,
preserved fruit and dry and pickled mushrooms are still
popular. So too are dumpling and noodle dishes. Modern
Polish cuisine offers imaginative, healthy derivatives of
traditional dishes. Salads and healthy snacks are popular,
and vegetarian dishes are now common in restaurants.

BREAKFAST

boczek bacon
boh • chehk
bułki rolls
boow • kee
chleb bread
hlehp
dżem jam
djehm
herbata tea
hehr • bah • tah

jajecznica *yah • yehch • n'ee • tsah*	scrambled eggs
jajka sadzone *yahy • kah sah • dzoh • nehs*	fried egg
jajko na twardo/miękko *yahy • koh nah tfahr • doh/myehnk • koh*	hard-boiled/ soft-boiled egg
jogurt *yoh • goort*	yogurt
kawa *kah • vah*	coffee
marmolada *mahr • moh • lah • dah*	marmalade
masło *mahs • woh*	butter
miód *myoot*	honey
mleko *mleh • koh*	milk
omlet *ohm • leht*	omelet
parówki *pah • roof • kee*	sausage
płatki śniadaniowe *pwaht • kee shn'yah • dah • n'yoh • veh*	cereal
ser *sehr*	cheese

Śniadanie (breakfast) is usually served between 07:00 and 10:00 a.m. **Obiad** (lunch) is the main meal, traditionally enjoyed between 1:00 and 5:00 p.m., but with changing working habits more and more people have their main meal in the evening. **Kolacja** (supper) is typically served from 6:00 p.m. onwards.

tost
tohst
toast

woda
voh•dah
water

APPETIZERS

grillowany oscypek
gree•loh•vah•nyh ohs•tsyh•pehk
grilled and smoked ewe's milk cheese

grzybki marynowane
gzhyhp•kee mah•ryh•noh•vah•neh
marinated wild mushrooms

naleśniki z kapustą i grzybami
nah•lehsh'•n'ee•kee skah•poos•tohm ee gzhyh•bah•mee
thin pancakes with sauerkraut and mushrooms

pieczarki w śmietanie
pyeh•chahr•kee fsh'myeh•tah•n'yeh
mushrooms in a cream sauce

sałatka
sah•waht•kah
mixed salad

sałatka jarzynowa
sah•waht•kah yah•zhyh•noh•vah
mixed vegetable salad in mayonnaise

sałatka pomidorowa z cebulą
sah•waht•kah poh•mee•doh•roh•vah stseh•boo•lohm
tomato and onion salad potato salad

sałatka ziemniaczana
sah•waht•kah zh'yehm•n'yah•chah•nah

śledź w oleju
sh'lehdj' voh•leh•yoo
herring in oil

śledź w śmietanie
sh'lehch' fsh'myeh•tah•n'yeh
herring in sour cream

węgorz wędzony
vehn•gohsh vehn•dzoh•nyh
smoked eel

SOUP

barszcz czerwony
bahrshch chehr • voh • nyh

bulion z pasztecikiem
bool • yohn spahsh • teh • ch'ee • kyehm

beet soup

consommé with
meat-filled
pastries

chłodnik z botwinki
hwohd • n'eek sboht • feen • kee

a cold soup with sour
cream, beets and
dill, served with
boiled eggs

grochówka
groh • hoof • kah

pea soup

jarzynowa
yah • zhyh • noh • vah

vegetable soup

kapuśniak
kah • poo • sh' • n'yahk

sauerkraut soup

ogórkowa
oh • goor • koh • vah

pickled cucumber
soup

pomidorowa z ryżem/makaronem
*poh • mee • doh • roh • vah z ryh • zhehm/
mah • kah • roh • nehm*

tomato soup with
rice/noodles

rosół (z kury)
roh • soow (skoo • ryh)

(chicken) broth

szczawiowa
shchah • vyoh • vah

sorrel soup with
boiled eggs

żurek (z białą kiełbasą)
*zhoo • rehk (zbyah • whom
kyehw • bah • sohm)*

sour rye soup (with
white sausage)

FISH & SEAFOOD

dorsz
dohrsh

cod

flądra
flohn • drah — flounder [plaice]

homar *hoh • mahr* — lobster

karp
kahrp — carp

karp po żydowsku
kahrp poh zhyh • doh • skoo — carp Jewish style: seasoned and cooked in beer fried carp

karp smażony
kahrp smah • zhoh • nyh — fried carp

krewetki
kreh • veht • kee — shrimp [prawns]

leszcz *lehshch* — bream

łosoś
woh • sohsh' — salmon

łupacz
woo • pahch' — haddock

makrela
mahk • reh • lah — mackerel

owoce morza
oh • voh • tseh moh • zhah — seafood

pstrąg
pstrohnk — trout

rak
rahk — crayfish

ryba
ryh • bah — fish

sandacz
sahn • dahch — perch

sandacz po polsku
sahn • dahch poh pohls • koo — perch in vegetable stock served with boiled eggs

śledź
sh'lehch' — herring

szczupak (faszerowany)   (stuffed) pike
shchoo • pahk (fah • sheh • roh • vah • nyh)

tuńczyk   tuna
toon' • chyhk

węgorz   eel
vehn • gohsh

MEAT & POULTRY

baranina   mutton
bah • rah • n'eeh • nah

bigos   sauerkraut with
bee • gohs   meat, prunes and
     mushrooms

boczek   bacon
boh • chehk

cielęcina   veal
ch'yeh • lehn' • ch'ee • nah

drób   poultry
droop

gęś   goose
gehn'sh'

gołąbki
goh • wohmp • kee

cabbage leaves stuffed with ground meat and rice

golonka
goh • lohn • kah

pork shank

gulasz wieprzowy
goo • lahsh vyehp • shoh • vyh

chopped pork with onions, pepper, garlic and tomato purée

indyk
een • dyhk

turkey

jagnię
yahg • n'yeh

lamb

kaczka
kahch • kah

duck

kaczka pieczona z jabłkami
kahch • kah pyeh • choh • nah zyahp • kah • mee

roast duck with apples

kiełbasa
kyehw • bah • sah

sausage

klopsy
klohp • syh

meatballs

kluski śląskie
kloos • kee sh'lohns • kyeh

Silesian dumplings

kotlety schabowe
koht • leh • tyh s • hah • boh • veh

breaded pork chops

kurczak
koor • chahk

chicken

mięso
myehn • soh

meat

ozór
oh • zoor

tongue

pierogi z...
pyeh • roh • gee z...

dumplings stuffed with...

  mięsem
  myehn • sehm

meat

schab pieczony ze śliwkami	roast pork loin with prunes
s • hahp pyeh • _choh_ • nyh zeh sh'leef • _kah_ • mee	
stek	steak
stehk	
szynka	ham
shyhn • kah	
wieprzowina	pork
vyehp • shoh • _vee_ • nah	
wołowina	beef
voh • woh • _vee_ • nah	
zrazy	rolled beef fillets
zrah • zyh	

VEGETABLES & STAPLES

bakłażan	eggplant [aubergine]
bahk • _wah_ • zhahn	
brokuł	broccoli
broh • _koow_	
brukselka	Brussel sprout
brook • _sehl_ • kah	
burak	beet
boo • rahk	
cebula	onion
tseh • _boo_ • lah	
cukinia	zucchini [courgette]
tsoo • _kee_ • n'yah	
czosnek	garlic
chohs • nehk	
fasolka szparagowa	green bean
fah • _sohl_ • kah shpah • rah • _goh_ • vah	
groszek	pea
groh • shehk	

jarzyna
yah • zhyh • nah

vegetable

kalafior
kah • lah • fyohr

cauliflower

kapusta
kah • poos • tah

cabbage

knedle ze śliwkami
knehd • leh zeh sh'leef • kah • mee

dumplings stuffed
with plums

leniwe pierogi
leh • n'ee • veh pyeh • roh • gee

large dumplings
made with flour,
potatoes and curd
cheese

marchew
mahr • hehf

carrot

mieszane jarzyny
myeh • shah • neh yah • zhyh • nyh

mixed vegetables

ogórek
oh • goo • rehk

cucumber

papryka
pahp • ryh • kah

pepper

pieczarka/grzyb
pyeh • chahr • kah/gzhyhb

mushroom/wild
mushroom

pierogi z...
pyeh • roh • gee z...

dumplings stuffed
with...

  grzybami
  gzhyh • bah • mee

mushrooms

  kapustą
  kah • poos • tohm

sauerkraut

  serem
  seh • rehm

curd cheese

  owocami
  oh • voh • tsah • mee

fruit

pierogi ruskie
pyeh • roh • gee roos • kyeh

potato and curd
cheese dumplings

placki ziemniaczane *plahts • keezyehm • n'yah • chah • neh*	potato pancakes
pomidor *poh • mee • dohr*	tomato
rzepa *zheh • pah*	turnip
sałata *sah • wah • tah*	lettuce
seler naciowy *seh • lehr nah • ch'yoh • vyh*	celery
ziemniak *z'yehm • n'yahk*	potato
chleb *hlehp*	bread
ryż *ryhsh*	rice
mąka (pszenna) *mohn • kah (pshehn • nah)*	(wheat) flour
makaron *mah • kah • rohn*	pasta
cukier *tsoo • kyehr*	sugar

FRUIT

agrest *ahg • rehst*	gooseberry
ananas *ah • nah • nahs*	pineapple
arbuz *ahr • boos*	watermelon
banan *bah • nahn*	banana
brzoskwinia *bzhohs • kfee • n'yah*	peach

cytryna
tsyh • tryh • nah

lemon

czereśnia
cheh • resh' • n'yah

cherry

grejpfrut
grehyp • froot

grapefruit

jabłko
yahp • koh

apple

limonka
lee • mohn • kah

lime

malina
mah • lee • nah

raspberry

morela
mo • reh • lah

apricot

owoce
oh • voh • tseh

fruit

pomarańcza
poh • mah • rahn' • chah

orange

porzeczka czarna/czerwona
poh • zhech • kah chahr • nah/
chehr • voh • nah

black/red currant

śliwka
sh'leef • kah

plum

truskawka
troos • kahf • kah

strawberry

winogrono
vee • noh • groh • noh

grape

CHEESE

biały ser
byah • wyh sehr

cottage cheese

bryndza
bryhn • dzah

ewe's milk cheese

camembert
kah • mehm • behr

camembert

ser
sehr

cheese

ser pleśniowy
sehr plehsh' • n'yoh • vyh

blue cheese

ser topiony
seh • ryh tohp • yoh • nyh

processed cheese

ser żółty
seh • ryh zhoow • tyh

hard cheese

twarożek
tfah • roh • zhehk

curd cheese

DESSERT

deser
deh • sehr

dessert

galaretka z bitą śmietaną
*gah • lah • reht • kah zbee • tohm
sh'myeh • tah • nohm*

fruit jelly with
whipped cream

gruszki w syropie
groosh • kee fsyh • roh • pyeh

pears in syrup

kompot owocowy
kohm • poht oh • voh • tsoh • vyh

fruit compote

lody... ...ice cream
loh • dyh...

  czekoladowe chocolate
  cheh • koh • lah • <u>doh</u> • veh

  malinowe raspberry
  mah • lee • <u>noh</u> • veh

  pistacjowe pistachio
  pees • tats • <u>yoh</u> • veh

  śmietankowe cream flavored
  sh'myeh • tahn • <u>koh</u> • veh •

  truskawkowe strawberry
  troos • kahf • <u>koh</u> • veh

  waniliowe vanilla
  vah • n'eel • <u>yoh</u> • veh

murzynek chocolate cake with
moo • <u>zhyh</u> • nek chocolate icing

naleśniki thin pancakes
nah • lesh' • <u>n'ee</u> • kee

owoce z bitą śmietaną fruit with whipped
oh • <u>voh</u> • tseh zbee • tohm cream
sh'myeh • <u>tah</u> • nohm

racuchy z jabłkami small fried pancakes
rah • <u>tsoo</u> • hyh z yahp • <u>kah</u> • mee made with sliced
apples

sernik cheesecake
<u>sehr</u> • n'eek

szarlotka apple tart
shahr • <u>loht</u> • kah

SAUCES & CONDIMENTS

keczup ketchup
<u>keh</u> • choop

majonez mayonaise
mah • <u>yoh</u> • nehs

musztarda　　　　　　　　　　mustard
moosh • <u>tahr</u> • dah

oliwa　　　　　　　　　　　　oil
oh • <u>lee</u> • vah

pieprz　　　　　　　　　　　pepper
<u>pyehpsh</u>

sól　　　　　　　　　　　　salt
sool

ocet　　　　　　　　　　　vinegar
<u>oh</u> • tseht

AT THE MARKET

Where are the carts [trolleys]/baskets?	**Gdzie są wózki/koszyki?** *gdj'yeh sohm <u>voos</u> • kee/koh • <u>shyh</u> • kee*
Where is/are…?	**Gdzie jest/są…?** *gdj'yeh yehst/sohm…*
I'd like some of that/ this…	**Poproszę trochę tego/tamtego…** *poh • <u>proh</u> • sheh troh • heh teh • goh/ tahm • teh • goh…*
Can I taste it?	**Mogę spróbować?** *<u>moh</u> • geh sproo • <u>boh</u> • vahch'*
More/Less.	**Trochę więcej/mniej.** *<u>troh</u> • heh <u>vyehn</u> • tsehy/mn'yehy*
How much?	**Ile to kosztuje?** *<u>ee</u> • leh toh kohsh • <u>too</u> • yeh*
I'd like…	**Poproszę…** *poh • <u>proh</u> • sheh…*
a kilo/ half-kilo of…	**kilo/pół kilo…** *<u>kee</u> • loh/poow <u>kee</u> • loh…*
a liter/ half-liter of…	**litr/pół litra…** *leetr/poow <u>leet</u> • rah…*
a piece of…	**kawałek…** *kah • <u>vah</u> • wehk…*

a slice of…	**plasterek…**
	plahs • teh • rehk…
Where do I pay?	**Gdzie się płaci?**
	gdj'yeh sh'yeh pwah • ch'ee
A bag, please.	**Poproszę torbę.**
	poh • proh • sheh tohr • beh
I'm being helped.	**Już jestem obsługiwany** *m/* **obsługiwana** *f.*
	joosh yehs • tehm
	ohp • swoo • gee • vah • nyh/
	ohp • swoo • gee • vah • nah

For Money, see page 31.

Measurements in Europe are metric – and that applies to the weight of food too. If you tend to think in pounds and ounces, it's worth brushing up on what the metric equivalent is before you go shopping for fruit and veg in markets and supermarkets. Five hundred grams, or half a kilo, is a common quantity to order, and that converts to just over a pound (17.65 ounces, to be precise).

YOU MAY HEAR...

Czym mogę służyć?
chyhm <u>moh</u> • geh <u>swoo</u> • zhyhch'

Can I help you?

Co dla pana?
tsoh dlah <u>pah</u> • nah

What would you like?

Coś jeszcze?
tsohsh' <u>yehsh</u> • cheh

Anything else?

To wszystko?
toh <u>fshyhs</u> • tkoh

Is that all?

(To będzie)...złotych.
(toh <u>behn</u> • dj'yeh)...<u>zwoh</u> • tyhh

(That's)...zlotys.

IN THE KITCHEN

bottle opener	**otwieracz do butelek**
	oht • <u>fyeh</u> • rahch doh boo • <u>teh</u> • lehk
bowl	**miska**
	<u>mees</u> • kah
can opener	**otwieracz do puszek**
	oht • <u>fyeh</u> • rahch doh <u>poo</u> • shehk
corkscrew	**korkociąg**
	kohr • <u>koh</u> • ch'yohnk
cup	**filiżanka**
	fee • lee • <u>zhahn</u> • kah
fork	**widelec**
	vee • <u>deh</u> • lehts
frying pan	**patelnia**
	pah • <u>tehl</u> • n'yah
glass (non-alcoholic/ alcoholic)	**szklanka/kieliszek**
	<u>shklahn</u> • kah/kyeh • <u>lee</u> • shehk
knife	**nóż**
	noosh

measuring cup/spoon	**miarka kuchenna/łyżka do odmierzania** _myahr_ • kah koo • _hehn_ • nah/_wyhsh_ • kah doh ohd • myeh • _zhah_ • n'yah
napkin	**serwetka** sehr • _veht_ • kah
plate	**talerz** _tah_ • lehsh
pot	**garnek** _gahr_ • nehk
saucepan	**rondel** _rohn_ • dehl
spatula	**łopatka** woh • _paht_ • kah
spoon	**łyżka** _wyhsh_ • kah
teaspoon	**łyżeczka** wyh • _zhehch`_ • kah

For Domestic Items, see page 79.

YOU MAY SEE…

NAJLEPIEJ SPOŻYĆ PRZED…	best if used by…
KALORIE	calories
BEZ TŁUSZCZU	fat free
PRZECHOWYWAĆ W LODÓWCE	keep refrigerated
MOŻE ZAWIERAĆ ŚLADOWE ILOŚCI…	may contain traces of…
SPRZEDAĆ PRZED	sell by

DRINKS

NEED TO KNOW

Can I see the wine list/ drink menu?	**Czy mogę prosić kartę win/listę drinków?**
	chyh moh • geh proh • sheech' kahr • teh veen/lees • teh dreen • koof
What do you recommend?	**Co może pan polecić?**
	tsoh moh • zheh poh • leh • ch'eech'
I'd like a bottle/glass of red/white wine.	**Poproszę butelkę/kieliszek czerwonego/białego wina.**
	poh • proh • sheh boo • tehl • keh/ kyeh • lee • shehk chehr • voh • neh • goh/ byah • weh • goh vee • nah
The house wine, please.	**Poproszę wino stołowe.**
	poh • proh • sheh vee • noh stoh • woh • veh
Another bottle/glass, please.	**Poproszę jeszcze jedną butelkę/ jeden kieliszek.**
	poh • proh • sheh yehsh • cheh jehd • nohm boo • tehl • keh/yeh • dehn kyeh • lee • shehk
I'd like a local beer.	**Poproszę lokalne piwo.**
	poh • proh • sheh loh • kahl • neh pee • voh
Can I buy you a drink?	**Mogę postawić panu drinka?**
	moh • geh pohs • tah • veech' pah • noo dreen • kah
Cheers!	**Na zdrowie!**
	nah zdroh • vyeh

A coffee/tea, please.	**Poproszę kawę/herbatę.**	
	poh • proh • sheh kah • veh/	
	hehr • bah • teh	
Black	**Czarną**	
	chahr • nohm	
A coffee with…, please.	**Poproszę kawę z…**	
	poh • proh • sheh kah • veh z…	
milk	**mlekiem**	
	mleh • kyehm	
sugar	**cukrem**	
	tsook • rehm	
artificial sweetener	**słodzikiem**	
	swoh • dj'ee • kyehm	
I'd like…	**Poproszę…**	
	poh • proh • sheh…	
a juice	**sok**	
	sohk	
a cola	**colę**	
	koh • leh	
a (sparkling/still) water	**wodę (gazowaną/niegazowaną)**	
	voh • deh (gah • zoh • vah • nohm/	
	n'yeh • gah • zoh • vah • nohm)	
Is the tap water safe to drink?	**Można pić wodę z kranu?**	
	mohzh • nah peech' voh • deh	
	skrah • noo	

NON-ALCOHOLIC DRINKS

cola   cola
koh • lah
gorąca czekolada   hot chocolate
goh • rohn • tsah cheh • koh • lah • dah

herbata... tea...
hehr • bah • tah...

  czarna black
  chahr • nah

  owocowa fruit
  oh • voh • tsoh • vah

  zielona green
  zh'yeh • loh • nah

  ziołowa herbal
  zh'yoh • woh • vah

  z cukrem with sugar
  stsook • rehm

  z cytryną with lemon
  stsyht • ryh • nohm

kawa... coffee...
kah • vah...

  z mlekiem with milk
  zmleh • kyehm

  z cukrem with sugar
  stsook • rehm

  czarna black
  chahr • nah

  bezkofeinowa decaffeinated
  behs • koh • feh • ee • noh • vah

  z ekspresu
  zehks • preh • soo espresso

  po turecku Turkish
  poh too • rehts • koo

lemoniada lemonade
leh • moh • n'yah • dah

mleko milk
mleh • koh

shake milk shake
shehyk

sok... ...juice
sohk...

  grejpfrutowy grapefruit
  grehyp • froo • toh • vyh

  pomarańczowy orange
  poh • mah • rahn' • choh • vyh

  jabłkowy apple
  yahp • koh • vyh

  owocowy juice
  sohk oh • voh • tsoh • vyh

  świeżo wyciskany fresh squeezed
  sh'fyeh • zho vyh • ch'ees • kah • nyh

woda gazowana/niegazowana sparkling/still water
voh • dah gah • zoh • vah • nah/
n'yeh • gah • zoh • vah • nah

Tea is a popular beverage in Poland, usually enjoyed black or with lemon. Traditionally, **esencja** (the essence) was brewed in a small ceramic teapot over a boiling kettle. The essence was poured into a glass or cup and then boiling water was added. Nowadays, tea bags are frequently used. Other types of tea, such as green, fruit or herbal tea, have become increasingly popular. Coffee is also popular, and many drink instant coffee at home. Specialty coffee, including espresso and mocha, is available at many of the numerous **kawiarnie** (coffee shops) in town.

YOU MAY HEAR...

Czy mogę postawić panu coś do picia?
Can I get you a drink?
chyh <u>moh</u> • geh pohs • tah • vich'
<u>pah</u> • noo tsosh' dohpee • ch'yah

Z mlekiem i z cukrem?
With milk and sugar?
z <u>mleh</u> • kyehm ee <u>stsook</u> • rehm

Gazowana czy niegazowana?
Sparkling or still water?
gah • zoh • <u>vah</u> • nah chyh n'yeh
gah • zoh • <u>vah</u> • nah

APERITIFS, COCKTAILS & LIQUEURS

ajerkoniak   egg-yolk liqueur
ah • yehr • <u>koh</u> • n'yahk

gin   gin
djeen

koniak   imported brandy
<u>koh</u> • n'yahk

miód pitny   mead
myoot <u>peet</u> • nyh

szarlotka   grass-flavored vodka
shahr • <u>loht</u> • kah   and apple juice

śliwowica   plum brandy
sh'lee • voh • <u>vee</u> • tsah

whisky   whisky
<u>wees</u> • kee

winiak   Polish brandy
<u>vee</u> • n'yahk

wódka...   vodka...
<u>voot</u> • kah...

  czysta   straight [neat]
  <u>chyhs</u> • tah

z lodem
z loh • dehm

on the rocks [with ice]

z wodą/tonikiem
z voh • dohm/ toh • n'ee • kyehm

with water/tonic water

żubrówka
zhoob • roof • kah

vodka flavored with bison grass

Vodka is one of the best known Polish exports. Several brands, such as Chopin® and Sobieski®, are very popular in the U.S. and U.K. However, the greatest Polish specialty is Żubrówka®, vodka flavored with a unique grass growing only in **Puszcza Białowieska** (Białowieża Forest) in eastern Poland. The grass lends Bison Vodka its unmistakeable taste and characteristic yellowish color. Vodka is served cold and enjoyed from small glasses or mixed with juice or soda. Flavored vodka is also popular.

Vodka, made from either potatoes or rye, is still the national drink, but beer has recently become equally popular. Polish beer includes Żywiec™, Tyskie™, Lech™ and Warka™; most well-known international brands can also be found.

BEER

piwo...
pee • voh...

beer...

bezalkoholowe
behz • ahl • koh • hoh • loh • veh

non-alcoholic

butelkowe/beczkowe
boo • tehl • koh • veh/ behch • koh • veh

bottled/draft [draught]

ciemne/jasne
ch'yehm • neh/yahs • neh

dark/light

jasne pełne	lager
yahs • neh pehw • neh	
lokalne	local
loh • kahl • neh	
pilsner	pilsner
peel • znehr	

WINE

wino...	...wine
vee • noh...	
białe	white
byah • weh	
czerwone	red
chehr • voh • neh	
deserowe	dessert
deh • seh • roh • veh	
musujące	sparkling
moo • soo • yohn • tseh	

ON THE MENU

ajerkoniak	liqueur made from
ah • yehr • koh • n'yahk	egg yolks, aromatic
	spirits, sugar, vanilla
	and brandy
agrest	gooseberry
ahg • rehst	
alkohol	alcohol
ahl • koh • hohl	
ananas	pineapple
ah • nah • nahs	
arbuz	watermelon
ahr • boos	

awokado
ah • voh • kah • doh

avocado

babeczka
bah • behch • kah

scone

bakłażan
bahk • wah • zhahn

eggplant [aubergine]

banan
bah • nahn

banana

baranina
bah • rah • n'ee • nah

mutton

baranina pieczona ze śmietaną
*bah • rah • n'ee • nah pyeh • choh • nah zeh
sh'myeh • tah • nohm*

roast mutton with
sour cream

barszcz (czerwony)
bahrshch (chehr • voh • nyh)

(red) beet [beetroot]
soup

bażant
bah • zhahnt

pheasant

bazylia
bah • zyhl • yah

basil

befsztyk tatarski
behf • shtyhk tah • tahrs • kee

steak tartare

beza
beh • zah

meringue

bezkofeinowa
behs • koh • feh • ee • noh • vah

decaffeinated

biała kapusta
byah • wah kah • poos • tah

white cabbage

białko
byahw • koh

egg white

biały ser
byah • wyh sehr

cottage cheese

bigos
bee • gohs

sauerkraut with
slices of meat, pork
sausage, prunes and
mushrooms

biszkopt
beesh • kohpt

sponge cake

bita śmietana
bee • tah sh'myeh • tah • nah

whipped cream

boczek
boh • chehk

bacon

brokuł
broh • koow

broccoli

brukiew
broo • kyehf

rutabaga [swede]

brukselka
brook • sehl • kah

Brussels sprout

bryndza
bryhn • dzah

ewe's milk cheese

brzoskwinia
bzhohs • kfee • n'yah

peach

budyń
boo • dyhn'

pudding

budyń z karmelem
boo • dyhn' skahr • meh • lehm

caramel pudding

bulion
boo • lyohn

clear soup

bułka
boow • kah
roll

bułka tarta
boow • kah _tahr_ • tah
bread crumbs

burak
boo • rahk
beet [beetroot]

cebula
tseh • _boo_ • lah
onion

chipsy
cheep • syh
chips [crisps]

chleb
hlehp
bread

chleb pszenny
hlehp _pshehn_ • nyh
wheat bread

chleb razowy
hlehp rah • _zoh_ • vyh
whole-wheat
[wholemeal] bread

chleb żytni
hlehp _zhyht_ • nee
rye bread

chłodnik
hwohd • n'eek
cold yogurt, dill and
beet [beetroot] soup

chrupki
hroop • kee
corn snacks

chrzan
hshahn
horseradish

ciasteczko
ch'yahs • _tehch_ • koh
cookie [biscuit]

ciasto
ch'yahs • toh
pastry, cake

ciasto francuskie
ch'yahs • toh frahn • _tsoos_ • kyeh
puff pastry

ciasto z bakaliami
ch'yahs • toh zbah • kahl • _yah_ • mee
dried fruit cake

ciecierzyca
ch'yeh • ch'yeh • _zhyh_ • tsah
chick pea

cielęcina
ch'yeh • lehn' • ch'ee • nah

veal

comber
cohm • behr

loin (usually game)

cukier
tsoo • kyehr

sugar

cukinia
tsoo • kee • n'yah

zucchini [courgette]

ćwikła
ch'feek • wah

horseradish with beets [beetroot]

cykoria
tsyh • koh • ryah

endive

cynamon
tsyh • nah • mohn

cinnamon

cytryna
tsyh • tryh • nah

lemon

czarna
chahr • nah

black (coffee)

czarna porzeczka
chahr • nah poh • zhehch • kah

black currant

czarny chleb
czahr • nyh hlehp

dark bread

czekolada
cheh • koh • lah • dah

chocolate

czereśnia
cheh • rehsh' • n'yah

cherry

czerwona fasola
chehr • voh • nah fah • soh • lah

kidney bean

czerwona kapusta
chehr • voh • nah kah • poos • tah

red cabbage

czerwone
chehr • voh • neh

red (wine)

czerwony pieprz
cher • voh • nyh pyehpsh

chilli pepper

czosnek _chohs • nehk_	garlic
daktyl _dahk • tyhl_	date
deser _deh • sehr_	dessert
domowy _doh • moh • vyh_	homemade
dorsz _dohrsh_	cod
drink _dreenk_	alcoholic drink
drób _droop_	poultry
dymka _dyhm • kah_	spring onion
dynia _dyh • n'yah_	pumpkin
dżem _djehm_	jam
dziczyzna _dj'ee • chyhz • nah_	game
dzik _dj'eek_	wild boar
estragon _ehs • trah • gohn_	tarragon
fasola _fah • soh • lah_	bean
fasolka szparagowa _fah • sohl • kah shpah • rah • goh • vah_	green bean
figa suszona/świeża _fee • gah soo • shoh • nah/sh'vyeh • zhah_	dried/fresh fig
flądra _flohn • drah_	flounder [plaice]

flaki
flah • kee
tripe

frytki
fryht • kee
French fries [chips]

galaretka
gah • lah • reht • kah
jelly

gałka muszkatołowa
gaw • kah moosh • kah • toh • woh • vah
nutmeg

gęś
gehn'sh'
goose

gęsty
gehns • tyh
rich (sauce)

gin z tonikiem
djeen stoh • nee • kyehm
gin and tonic

głowizna
gwoh • veez • nah
pig's head [brawn]

gołąbki
goh • whomp • kee
ground [minced] meat with rice rolled in cabbage leaves

golonka
goh • lohn • kah
pork shank

gorąca czekolada
goh • rohn • tsah cheh • koh • lah • dah
hot chocolate

gorzki
gohsh • kee
bitter

goździki
gozh' • djee • kee
cloves

grejpfrut
greyp • froot
grapefruit

grochówka
groh • hoof • kah
pea soup

groszek
groh • shehk
pea

groszek cukrowy
groh • shehk tsook • roh • vyh
sugarsnap pea

gruszka
groosh • kah

pear

gruszki w syropie
groosh • kee fsyh • roh • pyeh

pears in syrup

grzane wino
gzhah • neh vee • noh

mulled wine

grzyb
gzhyhb

wild mushroom

gulasz
goo • lahsh

meat stewed in gravy

gulasz wieprzowy
goo • lahsh vyep • shoh • vyh

pork stew

gulasz z jagnięcia
goo • lahsh zyahg • nyehn' • ch'yah

lamb stew

herbata
hehr • bah • tah

tea

herbatnik
hehr • baht • n'eek

biscuit

homar
hoh • mahr

lobster

imbir
eem • beer

ginger

indyk
een • dyhk

turkey

jabłko
yahp • koh

apple

jagnię
yahg • n'yeh

lamb

jagoda
yah • goh • dah

blueberry

jajecznica
yah • yehch • n'ee • tsah

scrambled eggs

jajko
yahy • koh

egg

jajko na miękko soft-boiled egg
yahy • koh nah myenk • koh

jajko na twardo hard-boiled egg
yahy • koh nah tfahr • doh

jajko sadzone fried egg
yahy • koh sah • dzoh • neh

jarzyna vegetable
yah • zhyh • nah

jeżyna blackberry
yeh • zhyh • nah

jogurt yogurt
yoh • goort

kabaczek marrow
kah • bah • chehk

kaczka duck
kahch • kah

kaczka pieczona z jabłkami roast duck with
kahch • kah apples
pyeh • choh • nah z yahp • kah • mee

kalafior cauliflower
kah • lah • fyohr

kałamarnica squid
kah • wah • mahr • n'ee • tsah

kanapka sandwich
kah • nahp • kah

kapary capers
kah • pah • ryh

kapuśniak sauerkraut soup
kah • poosh' • n'yahk

kapusta cabbage
kah • poos • tah

kapusta kiszona sauerkraut
kah • poos • tah kee • shoh • nah

karczoch artichoke
kahr • chohh

karp *kahrp*	carp
karp po żydowsku *kahrp poh zhyh • <u>dohs</u> • koo*	carp with spices cooked in beer
karp smażony *kahrp smah • <u>zhoh</u> • nyh*	fried carp
kaszanka *kah • <u>shahn</u> • kah*	black pudding
kasztan *kahsh • <u>tah</u> • nyh*	chestnut (sweet)
kawa *<u>kah</u> • vah*	coffee
kawa rozpuszczalna *<u>kah</u> • vah rohs • poosh • <u>chahl</u> • nah*	instant coffee
kawior *<u>kah</u> • vyohr*	caviar
kefir *<u>keh</u> • feer*	thin yogurt
kiełbasa *kyehw • <u>bah</u> • sah*	sausage
kiełbaska wieprzowa *kyehw • <u>bahs</u> • kah vyehp • <u>shoh</u> • vah*	pork sausage
kiełek fasoli *<u>kyeh</u> • wehk fah • <u>soh</u> • lee*	bean sprout
kisiel *<u>kee</u> • sh'ehl*	jelly
kiwi *<u>kee</u> • vee*	kiwi
klops *klohps*	meatball
kluski *<u>kloos</u> • kee*	noodles, dumplings
kluski śląskie *<u>kloos</u> • kee <u>sh'lohns</u> • kyeh*	Silesian dumplings

kminek	caraway
kmee • nehk	
knedle ze śliwkami	dumplings
stuffed_knehd • leh zeh shleef • kah • mee_	with plums
kokos	coconut
koh • kohs	
kompot	stewed fruit
kohm • poht	
koper	fennel
koh • pehr	
koperek	dill
koh • peh • rehk	
kopytka	small potato dumplings
koh • pyht • kah	
korniszon	gherkin
kohr • n'ee • shohn	
kość	bone
kohsh'ch'	
kotlet	chop
koht • leht	
kotlet schabowy	pork chop fried and
koht • leht s • hah • boh • vyh	breaded
kozie mleko	goat's milk
koh • zh'yeh mleh • koh	
krab	crab
krahp	
krakers	cracker
krah • kehrs	
krewetka	shrimp [prawn]
kreh • veht • kah	
krokiet	croquette
kroh • kyeht	
królik	rabbit
kroo • leek	

krupnik
kroop • neek
barley soup

kukurydza
koo • koo • _ryh_ • dzah
corn

kurczak
koor • chahk
chicken

kurczak grillowany
koor • chahk gree • loh • _vah_ • nyh
grilled chicken

kurczak pieczony
koor • chahk pyeh • _choh_ • nyh
roast chicken

kurczak smażony
koor • chahk smah • _zhoh_ • nyh
fried chicken

kurka
koor • kah
chanterelle mushroom

kuropatwa
koo • roh • _paht_ • fah
partridge

kwaśny
kfahsh´ • nyh
sour (taste)

łagodny
wah • _gohd_ • neh
mild (flavor)

langusta
lahn • _goos_ • tah
lobster

lekki
lehk • kee
light (sauce)

lemoniada
leh • moh • _n'yah_ • dah
lemonade

leniwe pierogi
leh • _n'ee_ • veh pyeh • _roh_ • gee
flour, potato and curd cheese dumplings

leszcz
lehshch
bream

likier
lee • kyehr
liqueur

limonka
lee • _mohn_ • kah
lime

liść laurowy	bay leaf
leesh'ch' lahw • roh • vyh	
lód	ice
loot	
lody	ice cream
loh • dyh	
łopatka	shoulder (cut of
woh • paht • kah	meat)
łosoś	salmon
woh • sohsh'	
łosoś wędzony	smoked salmon
woh • sohsh' vehn • dzoh • nyh	
lukier	icing
loo • kyehr	
łupacz	haddock
woo • pahch	
majonez	mayonnaise
mah • yoh • nehs	
majonez czosnkowy	garlic mayonnaise
mah • yoh • nehs chohsn • koh • vyh	
mąka	flour
mohn • kah	
mąka pszenna	wheat flour
mohn • kah pshehn • nah	
mąka razowa	whole-wheat
mohn • kah rah • zoh • vah	[wholemeal] flour
makaron	pasta
mah • kah • rohn	
makrela	mackerel
mahk • reh • lah	
malina	raspberry
mah • lee • nah	
małża	mussel
mahw • zhah	

mandarynka — tangerine
mahn • dah • ryhn • kah

marcepan — marzipan
mahr • tseh • pahn

marchew — carrot
mahr • hehf

margaryna — margarine
mahr • gah • ryh • nah

marmolada — marmalade
mahr • moh • lah • dah

marynowany w occie — marinated in vinegar
mah • ryh • noh • vah • nyh vohts • ch'yeh

maślanka — buttermilk
mahsh´ • lahn • kah

masło — butter
mahs • woh

mazurek — Easter shortcake
mah • zoo • rehk (various flavors)

melasa — molasses [treacle]
meh • lah • sah

melon — melon
meh • lohn

miecznik — swordfish
myehch • n'eek

mielona wołowina — minced beef
myeh • loh • nah voh • woh • vee • nah

mięso — meat
myehn • soh

mięso grillowane — grilled meat
myehn • soh gree • loh • vah • neh

mieszane jarzyny — mixed vegetables
myeh • shah • neh yah • zhyh • nyh

mięta — mint
myehn • tah

migdał
meeg • dahw
almond

migdały w cukrze
meeg • dah • wyh ftsook • sheh
sugared almonds

miód
myoot
honey

miód pitny
myoot peet • nyh
mead

mizeria
mee • zeh • ryah
cucumber salad with
sour cream

mleko
mle • koh
milk

młoda kapusta
mwoh • dah kah • poos • tah
spring cabbage

młody kurczak
mwoh • dyh koor • chahk
spring chicken

mocne
mohyts • neh
full-bodied (wine),
strong (beer)

morela
moh • reh • lah
apricot

morwa
mohr • vah
mulberry

mrożony
mroh • zhoh • nyh
iced (drinks)

mus
moos
mousse

musujący
moo • soo • yohn • tsyh
sparkling

musztarda
moosh • tahr • dah
mustard

naleśnik
nah • lehsh' • n'eek
thin pancake

naleśniki z kapustą i grzybami
*nah • lehsh' • n'ee • kee skah • poos • tohm
ee gzhyh • bah • mee*
thin pancakes
with sauerkraut
and mushrooms

napój
nah • puy

soft drink

nektarynka
nehk • tah • ryhn • kah

nectarine

nerka
nehr • kah

kidney

nerkówka
nehr • koof • kah

loin (cut of meat)

noga
noh • gah

leg (cut of meat)

nóżki
noosh • kee

pigs' feet

nugat
noo • gaht

nougat

ogon
oh • gohn

oxtail

ogórek
oh • goo • rehk

cucumber

ogórek kiszony
oh • goo • rehk kee • shoh • nyh

dill pickle

ogórek konserwowy
oh • goo • rehk kohn • sehr • voh • vyh

pickle

ogórkowa
oh • goor • koh • vah

pickled cucumber soup

okoń
oh • kohn'

bass

oliwka
oh • leef • kah

olive

oliwki nadziewane
oh • leef • kee nah • dj'yeh • vah • neh

stuffed olives

omlet
ohm • leht

omelet

opieniek
oh • pyeh • n'yehk

oyster mushroom

oranżada	orangeade
oh • rahn • zhah • dah	
orzech	nut
oh • zhehh	
orzech laskowy	hazelnut
oh • zhehh lahs • koh • vyh	
orzech nerkowca	cashew
oh • zhehh nehr • kohf • tsah	
orzech włoski	walnut
oh • zhehh vwohs • kee	
orzechy mieszane	assorted nuts
oh • zheh • hyh myeh • shah • neh	
orzeszek ziemny	peanut
oh • zheh • shehk zh'yehm • nyh	
orzeszki ziemne solone	salted peanuts
oh • zhehsh • kee zh'yehm • neh	
soh • loh • neh	
ośmiornica	octopus
ohsh' • myohr • nee • tsah	
ostra kiełbaska	spicy sausage
ohs • trah kyehw • bahs • kah	
ostry (smak)	hot, spicy (flavor)
ohs • tryh (smahk)	
ostryga	oyster
ohs • tryh • gah	
owoce	fruit
oh • voh • tseh	
owoce kandyzowane	candied fruit
oh • voh • tseh kahn • dyh • zoh • vah • neh	
owoce morza	seafood
oh • voh • tseh moh • zhah	
owoce z puszki	canned fruit
oh • voh • tseh spoosh • kee	
owsianka	porridge
ohf • sh'yahn • kah	

ozór   tongue
oh • zoor

pączek   donut [doughnut]
pohn • chehk

papryka zielona/czerwona   green/red pepper
_pahp • ryh • kah zh'yeh • loh • nah/
chehr • voh • nah_

parówka   sausage
pah • roof • kah

pasternak   parsnip
pah • stehr • nahk

paszteciki   pastries filled
pahsh • teh • ch'ee • kee   with meat, fish or
cabbage

pasztet   pâté
pahsh • teht

pasztet w galarecie   pâté in aspic
pahsh • teht vgah • lah • reh • ch'yeh

perliczka   guinea fowl
pehr • leech • kah

pieczarka   mushroom
pyeh • chahr • kah

pieczarki w śmietanie   mushrooms in cream
pyeh • chahr • kee vsh'myeh • tah • n'yeh

pieczeń   pot roast
pyeh • chehn'

pieczona wołowina   roast beef
pyeh • choh • nah voh • woh • vee • nah

pieprz   pepper (condiment)
pyehpsh

pieprzny sos   hot pepper sauce
pyehp • shnyh sohs

piernik   ginger cake
pyehr • n'eek

pierogi
pyeh • roh • gee

stuffed dumplings

pierogi ruskie
pyeh • roh • gee roos • kyeh

dumplings with
cheese and onion

pierogi z kapustą i z grzybami
*pyeh • roh • gee skah • poos • tohm ee
zgzhyh • bah • mee*

dumplings with
sauerkraut
and mushrooms

pierogi z mięsem
pyeh • roh • gee zmyehn • sehm

dumplings with meat

pierogi z owocami
pyeh • roh • gee zoh • voh • tsah • mee

dumplings with fruit

pierogi z serem
pyeh • roh • gee sseh • rehm

dumplings with curd
cheese

pierś
pyehrsh'

breast

pierś z kurczaka
pyehrsh' skoor • chah • kah

breast of chicken

pietruszka zielona
pyeht • roosh • kah zh'yeh • loh • nah

parsley

pikantny
pee • kahnt • nyh

spicy

piwo
pee • voh

beer

piwo jasne pełne
pee • voh yahs • neh pehw • neh

lager

placek
plah • tsehk

tart, pie

placki ziemniaczane
plahts • kee zh'yehm • n'yah • chah • neh

potato pancakes

płatki śniadaniowe
pwaht • kee sh'nyah • dah • n'yoh • veh

cereal

podroby
pohd • roh • byh

giblets

polędwica
poh • lehnd • vee • tsah

tenderloin (cut of
meat)

pomarańcza	orange
poh • mah • rahn' • chah	
pomidor	tomato
poh • mee • dohr	
pomidorowa z makaronem/ryżem	tomato soup with
poh • mee • doh • roh • vah z	noodles/ rice
mah • kah • roh • nehm/ryh • zhehm	
poncz	punch
pohnch	
por	leek
pohr	
porcja	portion
pohr • tsyah	
porto	port
pohr • toh	
potrawa	dish
poh • trah • vah	
potrawka	casserole
poh • trahf • kah	
prosiak	suckling pig
proh • sh'yahk	
przekąski	snacks
psheh • kohns • kee	
przepiórka	quail
psheh • pyoor • kah	
przyprawy	seasoning, spices
pshyh • prah • vyh	
przysmak regionalny	local specialty
pshyhs • mahk reh • gyoh • nahl • nyh	
pstrąg	trout
pstrohnk	
purée	purée
pee • reh	
purée z ziemniaków	potato purée
pee • reh zzh'yehm • n'yah • koof	

pyzy
pyh • zyh

large potato dumplings, sometimes with meat stuffing

rabarbar
rah • bahr • bahr

rhubarb

racuch
rah • tsooh

small pancake

racuchy z jabłkami
rah • tsoo • hyh zyahp • kah • mee

apple pancakes, fritters

rak
rahk

crayfish

rodzynki
roh • dzyhn • kee

raisins

rolmops
rohl • mohps

pickled herring filet [rollmop herring]

rosół
roh • soow

consommé, broth

rosół z kury
roh • soow skoo • ryh

chicken broth

rosół z mięsem i jarzynami
roh • soow zmyehn • sehm ee yah • zhyh • nah • mee

meat and vegetable broth

rostbef
rohst • behf

roast beef

rozmaryn
rohz • mah • ryhn

rosemary

rumsztyk
room • shtyhk

rumpsteak

ryba
ryh • bah

fish

ryż
rysh

rice

rzepa
zheh • pah

turnip

rzeżucha
zheh • zhoo • hah

cress

rzeżucha wodna
zheh • zhoo • hah vohd • nah

watercress

rzodkiewka
zhoht • kyehf • kah

radish

sałata
sah • wah • tah

lettuce

sałatka jarzynowa
sah • waht • kah yah • zhyh • noh • vah

mixed vegetable
salad

sałatka z kapusty
sah • waht • kah skah • poos • tyh

coleslaw

salceson
sahl • tseh • sohn

headcheese [brawn]

sandacz
sahn • dahch

perch

sandacz po polsku
sahn • dahch poh pohl • skoo

perch in vegetable
stock with eggs

sardela
sahr • deh • lah

anchovy

sardynka
sahr • dyhn • kah

sardine

sarnina
sahr • nee • nah

venison

schab
s • hahp

loin of pork

schab pieczony ze śliwkami
s • hahp pyeh • choh • nyh zeh sh'leef • kah • mee

roast pork sirloin
with prunes

schłodzony
s • hwoh • dzoh • nyh

chilled

seler naciowy
seh • lehr nah • ch'yoh • vyh

celery

ser
sehr

cheese

ser kozi
sehr koh • zh'ee

goat's cheese

ser owczy
sehr ohf • chyh

ewe's milk cheese

ser pleśniowy
sehr pleh • sh'n'yoh • vyh

blue cheese

ser topiony
sehr toh • pyoh • nyh

processed cheese

serce
sehr • tseh

heart

sernik
sehr • n'eek

cheesecake

shake
shehyk

milkshake

śledź
sh'lehch'

herring

śledź marynowany
sh'lehdj' mah • ryh • noh • vah • nyh

marinated herring

śledź w oleju
sh'lehdj' voh • leh • yoo

herring in oil

śledź w śmietanie
sh'lehch' fsh'myeh • tah • n'yeh

herring in sour cream

ślimak
sh'lee • mahk

snail

śliwka
sh'leef • kah

plum

śliwowica
sh'lee • voh • vee • tsah

plum brandy

słodka papryka
swoht • kah pah • pryh • kah

sweet red pepper

słodki
swoht • kee

sweet

słodycze
swoh • dyh • cheh

candies [sweets]

słodzik
swoh • dj'eek

sweetener

śmietana
sh'myeh • tah • nah

cream

soczewica
soh • cheh • vee • tsah

lentil

sok
sohk

juice

sok cytrynowy
sohk tsyh • tryh • noh • vyh

lemon juice

sok owocowy
sohk oh • voh • tsoh • vyh

fruit juice

sok pomarańczowy
sohk poh • mah • ran' • choh • vyh

orange juice

sok z limonki
sohk zlee • mohn • kee

lime juice

sól
sool

salt

sola
soh • lah

sole

solony
soh • loh • nyh

salted

sos
sohs

sauce

sos czosnkowy
sohs chohsn • koh • vyh

garlic sauce

sos pomidorowy
sohs poh • mee • doh • roh • vyh

tomato sauce

sos słodko-kwaśny
sohs swoht • koh • kfahsh' • nyh

sweet and sour sauce

sos winegret
sohs vee • neh • greh

vinaigrette [French dressing]

sos z pieczeni
sohs spyeh • cheh • n'ee

gravy

specjalność szefa kuchni special
*spehts • yahl • nohsh'ch' sheh • fah
kooh • n'ee*

stek steak
stehk

stek z polędwicy fillet steak
stehk spoh • lehnd • vee • tsyh

strucla strudel
stroots • lah

suflet soufflé
soof • leht

surówka fresh vegetable
soo • roof • kah salad

surowy raw
soo • roh • vyh

suszone daktyle dried dates
soo • shoh • neh dahk • tyh • leh

suszone śliwki prunes
soo • shoh • neh sh'leef • kee

świeże owoce fresh fruit
sh'fyeh • zheh oh • voh • tseh

świeży fresh
sh'fyeh • zhyh

świeży daktyl fresh date
sh'fyeh • zhyh dahk • tyhl

syrop syrup
syh • rohp

szafran saffron
shahf • rahn

szalotka shallot
shah • loht • kah

szałwia sage
shahw • vyah

szarlotka *shahr • loht • kah*	apple pie; grass-flavored vodka with apple juice
szaszłyk *shahsh • wyhk*	lamb or mutton kebab
szczaw *shchahf*	sorrel
szczawiowa zupa *shchah • vyoh • vah zoo • pah*	sorrel soup
szczupak *shchoo • pahk*	pike
szczupak nadziewany *shchoo • pahk nah • dj'yeh • vah • nyh*	stuffed pike
szczupak w galarecie *shchoo • pahk vgah • lah • reh • ch'yeh*	pike in aspic
szczypiorek *shchyh • pyoh • rehk*	chives
szklanka *shklahn • kah*	glass
sznycel *shnyh • tsehl*	breaded pork or veal cutlet
szparag *shpah • rahg*	asparagus
szpinak *shpee • nahk*	spinach
szprotka *shproht • kah*	sprat (small herring)
sztuka mięsa *shtoo • kah myehn • sah*	portion of meat
szynka *shyhn • kah*	ham
tłusty *twoos • tyh*	fatty (meat)
tonik *toh • neek*	tonic water

tort
tohrt

rich cake

tost
tohst

toast

trufla
troof • lah

truffle

truskawka
trus • kahf • kah

strawberry

tuńczyk
toon' • chyhk

tuna

twarożek
tfah • roh • zhehk

fresh curd cheese

tymianek
tyh • myah • nehk

thyme

udko
oot • koh

leg (cut of meat)

w cieście
fch'yehsh' • ch'yeh

in batter

w czosnku
fchohsn • koo

in garlic

w oliwie
voh • lee • vyeh

in olive oil

wafel
vah • felh

waffle

wanilia
vah • n'eel • yah

vanilla

wątróbka
vohn • troop • kah

liver

wątróbka z kurczaka
vohn • troop • kah skoor • chah • kah

chicken liver

wędlina
vehn • dlee • nah

cold cuts

węgorz
vehn • gohsh

eel

węgorz wędzony	smoked eel
vehn • gohsh vehn • dzoh • nyh	
wieprzowina	pork
vyehp • shoh • vee • nah	
winiak	Polish brandy
vee • n'yahk	
wino	wine
vee • noh	
wino deserowe	dessert wine
vee • noh deh • seh • roh • veh	
wino musujące	sparkling wine
vee • noh moo • soo • yohn • tseh	
wino stołowe	table wine
vee • noh stoh • woh • veh	
winogrono	grape
vee • noh • groh • noh	
winogrono czerwone	red grape
vee • noh • groh • noh chehr • voh • neh	
winogrono zielone	white grape
vee • noh • groh • noh zh'yeh • loh • neh	
wiśnia	cherry
veesh' • n'yah	
woda	water
voh • dah	
woda gazowana	sparkling water
voh • dah gah • zoh • vah • nah	
woda gorąca	hot water
voh • dah goh • rohn • tsah	
woda mineralna	mineral water
voh • dah mee • neh • rahl • nah	
woda niegazowana	still water
voh • dah n'yeh • gah • zoh • vah • nah	
woda sodowa	soda water
voh • dah soh • doh • vah	

woda z lodem _voh_ • dah _zloh_ • dehm	iced water
wódka _voot_ • kah	vodka
wódki _voot_ • kee	spirits
wół voow	ox
wołowina voh • woh • _vee_ • nah	beef
z cukrem _stsoo_ • krehm	with sugar
z cytryną stsyh • _tryh_ • nohm	with lemon
z kością _skohsh'_ • ch'yohm	on the bone
zając _zah_ • yohnts	hare
zakąski zah • _kohns_ • kee	appetizers
zapiekany zah • pyeh • _kah_ • nyh	gratin
zboże _zboh_ • zheh	grain
żeberka zheh • _behr_ • kah	spare ribs
zielona fasolka zh'yeh • _loh_ • nah fah • _sohl_ • kah	green bean
zielona sałata zh'yeh • _loh_ • nah sah • _wah_ • tah	lettuce
zielony pieprz zh'yeh • _loh_ • nyh pyehpsh	green pepper
ziemniak _zh'yehm_ • n'yahk	potato

ziemniak pieczony   baked potato
zh'yehm • n'yahk pyeh • choh • nyh

ziemniaki gotowane   boiled potatoes
zh'yehm • n'yah • kee goh • toh • vah • neh

zioła mieszane   mixed herbs
zh'yoh • wah myeh • shah • neh

zioło   herb
zh'yoh • woh

żółtko   egg yolk
zhoow • tkoh

żółty ser   hard cheese
zhoow • tyh sehr

Żubrówka   grass-flavoured vodka
zhoo • broof • kah

zupa   soup
zoo • pah

zupa jarzynowa   vegetable soup
zoo • pah yah • zhyh • noh • vah

zupa krem   cream soup
zoo • pah krehm

zupa na zimno   cold soup
zoo • pah nah zh'eem • noh

żurek (z białą kiełbasą)   sour rye soup (with white sausage)
zhoo • rehk (zbyah • wohm kyeh • bah • sohm)

PEOPLE

GOING OUT

NEED TO KNOW

What is there to do at night?	**Co można robić wieczorami?** *tsoh mohzh • nah roh • beech' vyeh • choh • rah • mee*
Do you have a program of events?	**Czy jest program imprez?** *chyh yehst proh • grahm eem • prehs*
What's playing at the movies [cinema] today?	**Co dzisiaj grają w kinie?** *tsoh dj'ee • sh'yay grah • yohm fkee • n'yeh*
Where's...?	**Gdzie jest...?** *gdj'yeh yehst...*
the downtown area	**centrum** *tsehn • troom*
the bar	**bar** *bahr*
the dance club	**dyskoteka** *dyhs • koh • teh • kah*

ENTERTAINMENT

Can you recommend…?	**Czy może pan polecić…?**
	chyh <u>moh</u> • zheh pahn poh • <u>leh</u> • ch'eech'…
a concert	**koncert**
	<u>kohn</u> • tsehrt
a movie	**film**
	feelm
an opera	**operę**
	oh • <u>peh</u> • reh
a play	**sztukę**
	<u>shtoo</u> • keh
When does it start/ end?	**Kiedy to się zaczyna/kończy?**
	<u>kyeh</u> • dyh toh sh'yeh zah • <u>chyh</u> • nah/ <u>kohn</u>' • chyh
I like…	**Lubię…**
	<u>loo</u> • byeh…
classical music	**muzykę poważną**
	moo • <u>zyh</u> • keh poh • <u>vahzh</u> • nohm
folk music	**muzykę ludową**
	moo • <u>zyh</u> • keh loo • <u>doh</u> • vohm
jazz	**jazz**
	djehz
pop music	**pop**
	pohp
rap	**rap**
	rahp
What's the dress code?	**Jaki strój obowiązuje?**
	<u>yah</u> • kee strooy oh • boh • vyohn • <u>zoo</u> • yeh

For Tickets, see page 45.

Most hotels will have some information available in English about events around town. There are also culture magazines, such as **Kalejdoskop Kulturalny** (Cultural Kaleidoscope), which have weekly events listings, often provided in Polish and English. These are available at newsstands and bookstores.

NIGHTLIFE

What is there to do at night?	**Co można robić wieczorami?** *tsoh mohzh nah roh beech' vyeh choh rah mee*
Can you recommend…?	**Czy może pan polecić…?** *chyh moh zheh pahn poh leh ch'eech'…*
a bar	**bar** *bahr*
a cabaret	**kabaret** *kah bah reht*
a casino	**kasyno** *kah syh noh*
a dance club	**dyskotekę** *dyhs koh teh keh*
a gay club	**klub dla gejów** *kloop dlah geh yoof*
a jazz club	**klub jazzowy** *kloop djeh zoh vyh*
a club with Polish music	**klub z polską muzyką** *kloop spohls kohm moo zyh kohm*
Is there live music?	**Czy grają muzykę na żywo?** *chyh grah yohm moo zyh keh nah zhyh voh*

How do I get there?	**Jak tam dotrzeć?**
	yahk tahm <u>doh</u> • tshehch'
Is there a cover charge?	**Czy płaci się za wstęp?**
	Chyh <u>pwah</u> • ch'ee sh'yeh zah vstehmp
Let's go dancing.	**Chodźmy potańczyć.**
	<u>hohch</u>' • myh poh • <u>tahn</u>' • chyhch'
Is this area safe at night?	**Czy ta okolica jest bezpieczna w nocy?**
	chyh tah oh • kho • lee • tsah yehst
	behs • py'eh • chnah vnoh • tsyh

For The Dating Game, see page 230.

YOU MAY HEAR...

Prosimy o wyłączenie telefonów komórkowych.	Turn off your cell [mobile] phones, please.
proh • <u>sh'ee</u> • myh oh	
vyh • wohn • <u>cheh</u> • n'yeh	
teh • leh • <u>foh</u> • noof koh • moor • <u>koh</u> • vyhh	

Dyskoteki (dance clubs) are popular throughout Poland. These feature a variety of music: dance, jazz, pop, etc. Prices are reasonable and many venues offer student discounts. At popular dance clubs you may need to make a reservation in advance.

ROMANCE

NEED TO KNOW

Would you like to go out for a drink/meal?	**Może pójdziemy na drinka/coś zjeść?** _moh • zheh pooy • dj'eh • myh nah dreen • kah/tsohsh' zyehsh'ch'_
What are your plans for tonight/tomorrow?	**Masz jakieś plany na wieczór/jutro?** _mahsh yah • kyehsh' plah • nyh nah vyeh • choor/yoot • roh_
Can I have your number?	**Podasz mi swój numer telefonu?** _poh • dahsh mee sfuy noo • mehr teh • leh • foh • noo_
Can I join you?	**Mogę się dosiąść?** _moh • geh sh'yeh doh • sh'yohn'sh'ch'_
Can I buy you a drink?	**Mogę postawić ci drinka?** _moh • geh pohs • tah • veech' ch'ee dree • nkah_
I like/love you.	**Lubię/Kocham cię.** _loo • bieh/koh • hahm ch'yeh_

THE DATING GAME

Would you like to go out for...?	**Może pójdziemy na...?** _moh • zheh pooy • dj'yeh • myh nah..._
coffee	**kawę** _kah • veh_
a drink	**drinka** _dreen • kah_
dinne	**kolację** _koh • lahts • yeh_

What are your plans for…?	**Masz jakieś plany na…?**
	mahsh yah • kyehsh' plah • nyh nah…
today	**dzisiaj**
	dj'ee • sh'yahy
tonight	**wieczór**
	vyeh • choor
tomorrow	**jutro**
	yoot • roh
this weekend	**weekend**
	wee • kehnt
Where would you like to go?	**Dokąd chciałbyś** m/**chciałabyś** f **pójść?**
	doh • kohnt hch'yahw • byhsh'/ hch'yah • wah • bysh' pooysh'ch'
I'd like to go to…	**Chciałbym** m/**Chciałabym** f **pójść do…** *hch'yahw • byhm/ hch'yah • wah • byhm pooysh'ch' doh…*
Do you like…?	**Lubisz…?**
	loo • beesh'…?
Can I have your number?	**Podasz mi swój numer telefonu?**
	poh • dahsh mee sfooy noo • mehr teh • leh • foh • noo
Can I have your e-mail?	**Podasz mi swój e-mail?**
	poh • dahsh mee sooy ee • mehyl
Are you on Facebook/Twitter?	**Masz konto na Facebooku/Twitterze?**
	mahsh kohn • toh nah fehys • boo • koo/ twee • teh • zheh
Can I join you?	**Mogę się dosiąść?**
	moh • geh sh'yeh doh • sh'yohn'sh'ch'
Is this seat free?	**To miejsce jest wolne?**
	toh myehys • tseh yehst vohl • neh
You look great!	**Świetnie wyglądasz!**
	sh'vyeht • n'yeh wyh • glohn • dahsh

You're very attractive **Jesteś bardzo atrakcyjny** m/
atrakcyjna f
yehs • tehsh' _bahr_ • dzoh
ah • trahk • _tsyhy_ • nyh/
ah • trahk • _tsyhy_ • nah

Let's go somewhere **Może pójdziemy w jakieś spokojniejsze**
quieter. **miejsce?**
moh • zheh puy • _dj'yeh_ • myh vyah • kyehsh'
spoh • kohy • _n'yehy_ • sheh _myehys_ • tseh

For Communications, see page 83.

ACCEPTING & REJECTING

I'd love to. **Bardzo chętnie.**
bahr • dzoh _chehnt_ • n'yeh

Where should we **Gdzie możemy się spotkać?**
meet? gdj'eh moh • _zheh_ • myh sh'yeh
spoht • kach'

I'll meet you at the **Spotkamy się w barze/twoim hotelu.**
bar/ your hotel. spoht • _kah_ • myh sh'yeh _vbah_ • zheh/
tfoh • eem hoh • _teh_ • loo

I'll come by at... **Przyjdę o...**
pshyhy • deh oh...

What's your address? **Gdzie mieszkasz?**
gdj'yeh _myehsh_ • kahsh

I'm busy. **Jestem zajęty** m/**zajęta** f
yehs • tehm zah • _yehn_ • tyh/zah • _yehn_ • tah

I'm not interested. **Nie jestem zainteresowany** m/
zainteresowana f
n'yeh yehs • tehm
zah • een • teh • reh • soh • _vah_ • nyh/
zah • een • teh • reh • soh • _vah_ • nah

Leave me alone, **Zostaw mnie w spokoju!**
please! _zohs_ • tahf mn'yeh fspoh • _koh_ • yoo

Stop bothering me! **Odczep się!**
oht • chehp sh'yeh

GETTING INTIMATE

Can I hug/kiss you?	**Mogę cię przytulić/pocałować?**
	moh • geh ch'yeh pshyh • too • leech'/
	poh • tsah • woh • vahch'
Yes.	**Tak.**
	tahk
No.	**Nie.**
	n'yeh
Stop!	**Przestań!**
	pshehs • tahn'
I love you	**Kocham cię**
	koh • hahm ch'yeh

SEXUAL PREFERENCES

Are you gay?	**Jesteś gejem** *m*/**lesbijką** *f* **?**
	yehs • tehsh' geh • yehm/lehs • beey • kohm
I'm…	**Jestem…**
	yehs • tehm…
heterosexual	**heteroseksualny** *m*/**heteroseksualna** *f*
	heh • teh • roh • sehk • soo • ahl • nyh/
	heh • teh • roh • sehk • soo • ahl • nah
gay	**gejem** *m*/**lesbijką** *f*
	geh • yehm/lehs • beey • kohm
bisexual	**biseksualny** *m*/**biseksualna** *f*
	bee • sehk • soo • ahl • nyh/
	bee • sehk • soo • ahl • nah
Do you like men/	**Wolisz mężczyzn/kobiety?**
women?	*voh • leesh mehnzh • chyhzn/*
	koh • byeh • tyh

DICTIONARY

ENGLISH–POLISH

A

a little trochę
a lot dużo
a.m. przed południem
accept v zaakceptować
accident (road) wypadek
accidentally przypadkowo
across przez
acrylic adj akrylowy; n akryl
actor aktor
adapter przejściówka
address adres
admission charge opłata za wstęp
adult n dorosły
afraid przestraszony
after (time) po; (place) za
afternoon popołudnie
aftershave płyn po goleniu
ago temu
agree zgadzać się
air conditioner klimatyzator
air conditioning klimatyzacja
air mattress materac nadmuchiwany
air pump kompresor

airline linia lotnicza
airmail poczta lotnicza
airport lotnisko
air-sickness bag torebka na chorobę lotniczą
aisle seat miejsce przy przejściu
alarm clock budzik
allergic uczulony
allergy uczulenie
allowance ilość
almost prawie
alone sam
already już
also również
alter poprawić
aluminum foil folia aluminiowa
always zawsze
amazing zdumiewający
ambassador ambasador
ambulance karetka
American adj amerykański; n Amerykanin
amount (money) kwota
and i
anesthetia znieczulenie

adj adjective	BE British English	prep preposition
adv adverb	n noun	v verb

animal zwierzę
another inny
antacid środek neutralizujący kwas
antibiotics antybiotyk
antique *n* antyk
antiseptic aseptyczny
antiseptic cream krem aseptyczny
any jakiś
anyone ktoś
apartment mieszkanie
apologize przepraszać
appendix wyrostek robaczkowy
appetite apetyt
appetizer przekąska
appointment (business) spotkanie; (doctor) wizyta
approximately około
arcade salon gier
area code numer kierunkowy
arm (body part) ramię
around (time) około; (place) po
arrive (car, train) przyjeżdżać; (plane) lądować
art gallery galeria sztuki
artist artysta
ashtray popielniczka
ask (question) pytać; (request) prosić
aspirin aspiryna
asthma astma

at (time) o; (place) na
ATM bankomat
attack atak
attractive atrakcyjny
audioguide przewodnik dźwiękowy
Australia Australia
authenticity autentyczność
automatic trasmission automatycza skrzynia biegów
autumn [BE] jesień
available (free) wolne
avalanche lawina

B

baby dziecko
baby food jedzenie dla dzieci
baby wipe wilgotne chusteczki pielęgnacyjne
babysitter opiekunka
back (head) tył; (body) grzbiet
backache ból grzbietu
backpack *n* plecak; *v* wędrować z plecakiem
bad zły
bag torba
baggage [BE] bagaż
baggage room przechowalnia bagażu
bakery piekarnia
balcony balkon
ball piłka
ballet balet
band (music) zespół

bandage bandaż
bank bank
bar bar
barber fryzjer męski
basement piwnica
basketball koszykówka
bath n wanna; v kąpiel
bathroom łazienka
battery bateria; **(car)** akumulator
battle site pole bitwy
be być
beach plaża
beautiful piękny
because ponieważ
bed łóżko
bedding pościel
bedroom sypialnia
before (time) przed
begin zaczynać
beginner początkujący
behind za
belong należeć
belt pasek
berth (ship) koja; **(train)** kuszetka
best najlepszy
better lepszy
between pomiędzy
bib śliniaczek
bicycle rower
bicycle route szlak rowerowy
big duży
bikini bikini
bill (restaurant) rachunek

binoculars lornetka
bird ptak
birthday urodziny
bite n ugryzienie
bitter gorzki
bizarre dziwaczny
black czarny
bladder pęcherz moczowy
bland mdły
blanket koc
bleach wybielacz
bleed krwawić
bleeding krwotok
blister pęcherz
block v blokować
blood krew
blood pressure ciśnienie krwi
blouse bluzka
blow-dry suszenie z modelowaniem
blue niebieski
board pokład
boarding card karta pokładowa
boat trip przejażdżka statkiem
boil v gotować
boiler boiler
bone kość
book książka
bookstore księgarnia
boots botki
boring nudny
born v urodzić się

borrow pożyczyć

botanical garden ogród botaniczny

bottle butelka

bottle opener otwieracz do butelek

bowl miska

box (container) pudełko

boy chłopiec

boyfriend chłopak

bra biustonosz

bracelet bransoletka

brake hamulec

break (destroy) zepsuć; **(body part)** złamać

break down (go wrong) zepsuć się

breakfast śniadanie

breast (body) pierś

breathe oddychać

bridge most

briefs (clothing) majtki

bring przenieść

Britain Wielka Brytania

British *adj* brytyjski; *n* Brytyjczyk

brochure broszura

broken zepsuty

bronchitis bronchit

brooch broszka

brother brat

browse patrzeć

bruise siniak

bucket wiaderko

bug robak

build budować

building budynek

bulletin board tablica informacyjna

burn *n* oparzenie

bus autobus

bus route trasa autobusowa

bus station dworzec autobusowy

bus stop przystanek autobusowy

business biznes

business class klasa biznes

busy zajęty

but ale

butane gas butan

butcher (store) rzeźnik

button guzik

buy kupić

C

cabaret kabaret

café kawiarnia

call (ambulance) wezwać; **(telephone)** zadzwonić

camera aparat fotograficzny

camera case futerał na aparat

camp *n* obóz; *v* obozować

campfire ognisko

campsite pole namiotowe

can *n* puszka; *v* móc

can opener otwieracz do puszek

Canada Kanada

canal kanał

cancel odwołać
cancer rak
cap (dental) koronka; **(clothing)** czapka
car samochód; **(train)** wagon
car hire [BE] wynajem samochodów
car insurance ubezpiecznie samochodowe
car park parking
car rental wynajem samochodów
car seat fotelik dziecięcy
carafe karafka
card karta
careful ostrożny
carpet dywan
carry-on (luggage) bagaż podręczny
cart wózek
carton karton
cash (money) gotówka; *v* zrealizować
cashier kasjer
casino kasyno
castle zamek
catch (bus) złapać
cathedral katedra
cave jaskinia
CD płyta
CD player odtwarzacz płyt kompaktowych
cell phone telefon komórkowy

cemetery cmentarz
ceramics ceramika
certificate certyfikat
chain łańcuszek
change *n* **(small coins)** drobne; **(in shop)** reszta; *v* **(bus, train)** przesiadać się; **(baby)** przewinąć; **(money)** wymieniać; **(reservation)** zmienić, **(clothes)** przebrać się
changing room przebieralnia
charcoal węgiel drzewny
charge opłata
cheap tani
check *n* czek
check in *n* odprawa
check out (hotel) wyrejestrować się
checkbook książeczka czekowa
check-in desk stanowisko odprawy
chemical toilet chemiczna toaleta
chemist [BE] apteka
cheque [BE] czek
chess szachy
chest (body) klatka persiowa
child dziecko
child's cot łóżeczko dziecięce
child's seat krzesełko dla

dziecka

church kościół

cigar cygaro

cigarette papieros

clamp założyć blokadę na koła

clean adj czysty; v wyczyścić

cliff klif

cling film [BE] folia do żywności

clinic klinika

clock zegar

close (near) niedaleko; **(store)** zamykać

clothing store sklep odzieżowy

cloudy pochmurno

coach [BE] **(long-distance bus)** autokar

coat płaszcz

coat check szatnia

coat hanger wieszak

cockroach karaluch

coin moneta

cold adj zimny; adv zimno; n **(illness)** przeziębienie

collapse upaść

collect zebrać

collect call rozmowa na koszt rozmówcy

color kolor

color film film kolorowy

comb grzebień

come przyjść

come back (return) wrócić

commission prowizja

company (companionship) towarzystwo; **(business)** firma

compartment (train) przedział

composer kompozytor

computer komputer

concert koncert

concert hall sala koncertowa

concession koncesja

concussion wstrząs mózgu

conditioner odżywka

condom prezerwatywa

conductor dyrygent

confirm potwierdzić

confirmation potwierdzenie

connect (internet) połączyć się z siecią

connection (train) połączenie

conscious (awake) przytomny

constant ciągły

constipation zaparcie

consulate konsulat

consult skonsultować się

contact skontaktować się

contact lens szkło kontaktowe

contagious zakaźny

contain zawierać

contraceptive środek antykoncepcyjny

convenience store sklep osiedlowy

cook v gotować; n kucharz

cooker [BE] kuchenka

cooking (cuisine) kuchnia

cooking facilities możliwość gotowania

copper miedź

copy kopia

corkscrew korkociąg

correct prawidłowy

cosmetics kosmetyki

cost v kosztować

cot rozkładane łóżko

cottage domek

cotton (material) bawełna

cough n kaszel; v kaszleć

country kraj

country code numer kierunkowy

country music muzyka country

course (meal) danie; **(path)** droga

cousin kuzyn

cramp skurcz

credit card karta kredytowa

credit card number numer karty kredytowej

crib łóżeczko dziecięce

cross v przejść

cross-country skis biegówki

crowd tłok

crowded zatłoczony

crown (dental) koronka; **(royal)** korona

cruise n rejs

crystal (quartz) kryształ

cup filiżanka

cupboard szafka kuchenna

currency waluta

currency exchange office kantor

currency exchange rate kurs wymiany

curtain zasłona

customs urząd celny

customs declaration deklaracja celna

cut (hair) strzyżenie; **(wound)** rana cięta

cut glass cięte szkło

cutlery sztućce

cycling kolarstwo

D

daily adj codzienny; adv codziennie

damaged zniszczony

damp adj wilgotny

dance n taniec; v tańczyć

dance club dyskoteka

dangerous niebezpieczny

dark ciemny

daughter córka

dawn świt

day dzień

day charge opłata za dzień

day ticket bilet jednodniowy

day trip wycieczka jednodniowa

dead (battery) wyczerpany

deaf głuchy

deck chair leżak

declare zadeklarować

deduct odejmować

deep głęboki

defrost rozmrozić

degree (temperature) stopień

delay opóźnienie

delayed opóźniony

delicatessen delikatesy

delicious smaczny

deliver dostarczyć

delivery dostawa

denim drelich

dental floss nić dentystyczna

dentist dentysta

denture proteza dentystyczna

deodorant dezodorant

depart (train, bus) odjeżdżać; (plane) startować

department store dom towarowy

departure lounge poczekalnia

departures (airport) hala odlotów

deposit (security) kaucja

describe opisać

description opis

destination (travel) cel podróży

detail szczegół

detergent środek czystości

develop (photos) wywołać

diabetes cukrzyca

diabetic n cukrzyk

dialing code numer kierunkowy

diamond brylant

diaper pieluszka

diarrhea biegunka

dice kostka do gry

dictionary słownik

diesel diesel

diet dieta

difficult trudny

dining car wagon restauracyjny

dining room jadalnia

dinner kolacja

direct adj (train, journey) bezpośredni; v (to a place) wskazać kierunek

direction kierunek

director (company) dyrektor

directory (telephone) książka telefoniczna

dirty brudny

disabled n niepełnosprawny

discount zniżka

discount card karta rabatowa

dish (meal) danie

dishcloth ścierka

dishwasher zmywarka

dishwashing liquid płyn do zmywania

display cabinet gablota

display case gablota

disposable camera aparat jednorazowy

disturb przeszkadzać

dive (scuba dive) nurkować;

(jump) skakać

diving equipment sprzęt do nurkowania

divorced rozwiedziony

dizziness zawroty głowy

do robić

doctor lekarz

doll lalka

dollar dolar

domestic (flight) krajowy

door drzwi

double bed podwójne łóżko

double room pokój dwuosobowy

downtown area centrum

dozen tuzin

dress sukienka

drink *n* **(alcoholic)** drink; *v* pić

drink menu lista drinków

drip ciec

drive jechać

driver (car) kierowca

driver's license prawo jazdy

drown tonąć

drugstore drogeria

drunk pijany

dry cleaner's pralnia chemiczna

dry-clean czyścić (chemicznie)

dubbed dubbingowany

dummy [BE] smoczek

during podczas

dustbin [BE] śmietnik

duty cło

duvet kołdra

E

ear ucho

ear drops krople do uszu

earache ból ucha

early *adj* wczesny; *adv* wcześnie

earring kolczyk

east wschód

easy łatwy

eat jeść

economy class klasa turystyczna

elastic *adj* elastyczny

electric shaver golarka elektryczna

electrical outlet gniazdko elektryczne

electronic elektroniczny

elevator winda

e-mail *n* e-mail; *v* napisać maila

e-mail address adres e-mail

embassy ambasada

embroidery haft

emerald szmaragd

emergency nagły wypadek

emergency exit wyjście awaryjne

emergency ward izba przyjęć

empty pusty

enamel emalia

end *n* koniec; *v* kończyć (się)

engaged zaręczony

engine silnik
engineer inżynier
England Anglia
English *adj* angielski; *n* Anglik
enjoy podobać się
enjoyable przyjemny
enlarge (photos) powiększyć
enough dość
entertainment guide program rozrywek
entrance fee opłata za wstęp
envelope koperta
epilepsy epilepsja
epileptic *n* epileptyk
equipment (sports) sprzęt
era epoka
error błąd
escalator schody ruchome
escape route droga ewakuacyjna
essential niezbędny
e-ticket bilet elektroniczny
eurocheque euroczek
European Union Unia Europejska
evening wieczór
evening dress strój wieczorowy
every każdy
examination (medical) badanie
example przykład
except oprócz
excess baggage nadbagaż
exchange wymienić

exchange rate kurs wymiany
excursion wycieczka
exhausted wyczerpany
exit wyjście
expensive drogi
experienced zaawansowany
expiration date data ważności
expiry date [BE] data ważności
exposure (photos) naświetlanie
express ekspres
express mail priorytet
extension (phone) wewnętrzny
extra (additional) dodatkowy
extract (tooth) wyrwać
eye oko

F

fabric materiał
face twarz
facial zabieg oczyszczania skóry
faint *v* zemdleć
fairground wesołe miasteczko
fall *n* jesień
family rodzina
famous sławny
fan (electric) wentylator
far daleko
farm gospodarstwo
far-sighted dalekowidz
fast szybko

father ojciec

faucet kran

faulty wadliwy

favorite ulubiony

fax faks

fee opłata

feed nakarmić

feel czuć (się)

female kobieta

ferry prom

fever gorączka

few parę

fiancé narzeczony

fiancée narzeczona

field pole

fight (brawl) bójka

fill out (a form) wypełnić

fill up (car) nalać do pełna

filling (dental) plomba

film (camera, movie) film

filter filtr

find znaleźć

fine (well) dobrze; **(penalty)** grzywna

finger palec

fire pożar

fire alarm alarm pożarowy

fire brigade [BE] straż pożarna

fire department straż pożarna

fire door drzwi przeciwpożarowe

fire escape schody pożarowe

fire exit wyjście awaryjne

fire extinguisher gaśnica

first class pierwsza klasa

first floor parter

fish store sklep rybny

fit v pasować

fitting room przymierzalnia

fix v naprawić

flame płomień

flashlight latarka

flat (tire) przebity

flavor smak

flea pchła

flea market pchli targ

flight lot

flight number numer lotu

floor (level) piętro

florist kwiaciarnia

flower kwiat

flu grypa

flush (toilet) spuszczać wodę

fly n mucha; v latać

fog mgła

folk art sztuka ludowa

folk music muzyka ludowa

follow (pursue) podążać; **(road, sign)** jechać zgodnie z

food jedzenie

food poisoning zatrucie pokarmowe

foot stopa

football [BE] piłka nożna

footpath [BE] dróżka

for (time) przez; **(duration)** na

foreign currency obca waluta

forest las

forget zapominać

fork widelec
form formularz
formal dress strój formalny
fortunately na szczęście
fountain fontanna
foyer (hotel, theater) foyer
fracture złamanie
frame (glasses) oprawka
free (available) wolny;
  (without charge) bezpłatny
freezer zamrażarka
frequently często
fresh świeży
friend przyjaciel
friendly (person) przyjazny;
  (place, atmosphere)
  przyjemny
frightened przerażony
from (place) z; **(time)** od
front przód
frost mróz
frying pan patelnia
fuel paliwo
full pełny
full board z pełnym
  wyżywieniem
fun zabawa
funny śmieszny
furniture meble

G

gallon galon
game gra; **(sports)** mecz
garage (mechanic) warsztat
  samochodowy; **(parking lot)**
  garaż
garbage śmieci
garbage bag worek na śmieci
garden ogródek
gas (fuel) benzyna
gas station stacja benzynowa
gate (airport) wyjście
gauze gaza
genuine prawdziwy
get (buy) kupić; **(find)** znaleźć
get back (return) wrócić
get off (bus/train) wysiąść
get to dojechać do
gift prezent
gift shop sklep z upominkami
giftwrap zapakować na
  prezent
girl dziewczyna
girlfriend dziewczyna
give dać
glass (non-alcoholic)
  szklanka; **(alcoholic)**
  kieliszek
glasses (optical) okulary
glove rękawiczka
go (on foot) iść; **(by bus,
  train)** jechać; **(by plane)**
  lecieć
go away odejść
goggles (swimming) okularki;
  (skiing) gogle
gold złoto
golf golf
golf club kij golfowy
golf course pole golfowe

good dobry
good evening dobry wieczór
good morning dzień dobry
good night dobranoc
goodbye do widzenia
gram gram
grandfather dziadek
grandmother babcia
grandparents dziadkowie
grass trawa
gray szary
great *adj* świetny; *adv* świetnie
green zielony
greengrocer [BE] warzywniak
grocery store sklep spożywczy
ground (earth) ziemia
ground floor [BE] parter
groundcloth podłoga namiotu
groundsheet [BE] podłoga namiotu
group grupa
group guide przewodnik grupowy
group leader kierownik grupy
group ticket bilet grupowy
guarantee gwarancja
guest gość
guesthouse pensjonat
guide (tour) przewodnik
guidebook przewodnik
guided tour wycieczka z przewodnikiem
guided walk wycieczka piesza z przewodnikiem
guitar gitara

gym siłownia
gynecologist ginekolog

H

hair włosy
hair gel żel do włosów
haircut strzyżenie włosów
hairdresser fryzjer
hairspray lakier do włosów
half pół
hammer młotek
hand ręka
hand luggage [BE] bagaż podręczny
hand washable prać ręcznie
handbag torebka
handicapped niepełnosprawny
handicrafts wyroby rękodzielnicze
handkerchief chusteczka
hanger wieszak
hangover *n* kac
happy szczęśliwy
harbor port
hard (texture) twardy; **(difficult)** ciężki
hat kapelusz
have mieć
hay fever katar sienny
head *n* głowa; *v* **(go towards)** jechać w kierunku
head waiter kierownik sali
headache ból głowy
health zdrowie

health food store sklep ze zdrową żywnością
health insurance ubezpieczenie zdrowotne
hear słyszeć
hearing aid aparat słuchowy
heart serce; (cards) kier
heart attack zawał serca
heat ogrzewanie
heater grzejnik
heating [BE] ogrzewanie
heavy ciężki
height wzrost
helmet kask
help pomoc
hemorrhoids hemoroidy
her jej
here tutaj
hernia przepuklina
herpes opryszczka
hers jej
high wysoki
highchair wysokie krzesełko
highlight v (hair) robić pasemka; (stress) podkreślić
highway autostrada
hiking (general) turystyka piesza; (trip) wędrówka
hill wzgórze
him niego
hire [BE] v wynająć
his jego
historic site miejsce historyczne

hobby (pastime) hobby
holiday [BE] wakacje
holiday resort miejscowość wypoczynkowa
home (be/go) w domu/do domu
honeymoon miesiąc miodowy
horse koń
horse racing wyścigi konne
hospital szpital
hot gorący
hot spring gorące źródło
hotel hotel
hour godzina
house dom
housewife gospodyni domowa
hundred sto
hungry głodny
hurt boleć
husband mąż

I

ice-cream parlor lodziarnia
icy oblodzony
identification dowód tożsamości
ill chory
illegal nielegalny
imitation imitacja
in (place) w; (period of time) w ciągu
included wliczony
incredible niewiarygodny

indicate wskazywać
indigestion niestrawność
indoor pool kryty basen
inexpensive niedrogi
infected zakażony
infection infekcja
inflammation zapalenie
informal (dress) nieformalny
information (desk, office)
  infomacja
injection zastrzyk
injured ranny
innocent niewinny
insect insekt
insect bite ugryzienie owada
insect repellent środek na
  owady
insect sting użądlenie
inside w środku
insist nalegać
insomnia bezsenność
instead zamiast
instruction instrukcja
instructor instruktor
insulin insulina
insurance ubezpieczenie
insurance card polisa
  ubezpieczeniowa
insurance certificate [BE]
  polisa ubezpieczeniowa
insurance claim wniosek o
  odszkodowanie
interest (hobby)
  zainteresowanie
interested zainteresowany

interesting interesujący
international (flight)
  międzynarodowy
International Student Card
  Międzynarodowa Karta
  Studenta
internet internet
internet cafe kafejka
  internetowa
interpreter tłumacz ustny
intersection skrzyżowanie
into do
intolerance nietolerancja
invite zaprosić
iodine jodyna
Ireland Irlandia
iron *n* żelazko; *v* prasować
itch swędzieć
item (object) przedmiot
itemized bill szczegółowy
  rachunek

J

jacket (men's) marynarka;
  (women's) żakiet
jaw szczęka
jazz jazz
jeans dżinsy
jellyfish meduza
jet-ski skuter wodny
jeweler jubiler
jewelry biżuteria
join (a group) dołączyć się
joint (body) staw
joke żart

journalist dziennikarz
journey podróż
jug (water) dzbanek
jumper [BE] pulower
junction [BE] (intersection) skrzyżowanie

K

keep zatrzymać
kerosene nafta
kettle czajnik
key klucz
key card (hotel) karta
kiddie pool brodzik
kidney nerka
kilometer kilometr
kind *adj* uprzejmy; *n* rodzaj
kiss *n* pocałunek; *v* całować
kitchen kuchnia
kitchen foil [BE] folia aluminiowa
knee kolano
knickers [BE] majtki
knife nóż
know wiedzieć
kosher koszerny

L

label (sticker) nalepka; **(on bottle)** etykieta
lace koronka
ladder drabina
lake jezioro
lamp lampa
land *v* lądować

language course kurs językowy
large (size) duży
last *adj* ostatni; **(previous)** zeszły; *v* trwać
late (not early) późny; **(delayed)** opóźniony
later później
laundromat pralnia samoobsługowa
laundry facilities pralnia
lawyer prawnik
laxative środek przeczyszczający
lead *n* smycz; *v* prowadzić
leader (ideological) przywódca; **(manager)** menedżer
leak *n* przeciek; *v* **(roof, pipe)** przeciekać
learn (language) uczyć się
leather skóra
leave (depart) odjeżdżać; **(deposit)** zostawić; **(on foot)** odejść; **(depart of plane)** odlatywać
left *adj* lewy
left-luggage office [BE] przechowalnia bagażu
leg noga
legal legalny
lend pożyczyć
lens (optical) soczewka; **(camera)** obiektyw
lense cap nakładka na

obiektyw
less mniej
lesson lekcja
let v (permit) pozwolić
let go puścić
letter list
library biblioteka
license plate number numer rejestracyjny
life preserver koło ratunkowe
lifeboat łódź ratunkowa
lifeguard ratownik
lifejacket kamizelka ratunkowa
lift [BE] winda
lift pass (skiing) skipass
light adj (weight) lekki; (color) jasny; n światło
light bulb żarówka
lighter adj jaśniejszy; n zapalniczka
like v lubić
limousine limuzyna
line (metro) linia metra
linen len
lip warga
lipgloss błyszczyk
lipstick szminka
liquor store sklep monopolowy
liter litr
little (small) mały
live mieszkać
liver wątroba
living room salon

lobby (theater) foyer; (hotel) hol
local lokalny
lock n (door) zamek; (bike) blokada; v zamknąć
log off wylogować się
log on zalogować się
login login
long długi
long-distance bus autokar
long-sighted [BE] dalekowidz
loose luźny
lorry [BE] ciężarówka
lose (item) zgubić; (person) stracić
lost-and-found biuro rzeczy znalezionych
lost-property office [BE] biuro rzeczy znalezionych
love n miłość; v kochać
lovely śliczny
low niski
lower (berth) dolny
low-fat o niskiej zawartości tłuszczu
luck szczęście
luggage bagaż
luggage cart wózek na bagaż
luggage locker schowek na bagaż
luggage trolley [BE] wózek na bagaż
lump guz
lunch obiad
lung płuco

M

machine washable prać w pralce
madam pani
magazine czasopismo
magnificent wspaniały
maid pokojówka
mail *n* poczta; *v* wysłać
mailbox skrzynka pocztowa
main główny
make zrobić
male mężczyzna
mallet młotek drewniany
manager menadżer
manicure manicure
many dużo
map mapa
market (job market) rynek; (place to buy) targ
married żonaty
mascara tusz do rzęs
mask (diving) maska
mass msza
massage masaż
match (game) mecz; (light) zapałka
mattress materac
maybe może
me ja
meal posiłek
measles odra
measure zmierzyć
measurement miara
measuring cup miarka

kuchenna
measuring spoon łyżka do odmierzania
mechanic mechanik
medication lek
medicine lekarstwo
medium średni
meet (get to know) poznać; (appointment) spotkać
meeting place miejsce zbiórki
meeting point [BE] miejsce zbiórki
member (association) członek
memorial (war) pomnik
mention wspominać
menu menu
message wiadomość
metal metal
metro map mapa metra
metro station stacja metra
microwave (oven) kuchenka mikrofalowa
midday [BE] południe
midnight północ
migraine migrena
million milion
mine mój
mini-bar mini-bar
minute (time) minuta
mirror lustro
miss (lack) brakować; (lost) zaginąć
mistake błąd
misunderstanding

nieporozumienie
mobile home przyczepa mieszkalna
mobile phone [BE] telefon komórkowy
moisturizer (cream) krem nawilżający
monastery klasztor
money pieniądze
money order przekaz pieniężny
month miesiąc
monument pomnik
mop mop
moped motorower
more więcej
morning rano
mosque meczet
mosquito bite ukąszenie komara
mother matka
motion sickness choroba lokomocyjna
motorbike motor
motorboat motorówka
motorcycle motor
motorway [BE] autostrada
mountain góra
mountain bike rower górski
mountain pass przełęcz górska
mountain range łańcuch górski
moustache wąsy
mouth usta

move ruszać
movie film
movie theater kino
much dużo
mug *n* kubek; *v* napadać
mugging napad
mumps świnka
muscle mięsień
museum muzeum
music muzyka
music store sklep muzyczny
musician muzyk
must *v* musieć
my mój

N

name imię
napkin serwetka
nappy [BE] pieluszka
narrow wąski
national narodowy
national park park narodowy
nationality obywatelstwo
native tutejszy
nature reserve rezerwat przyrody
nature trail szlak przyrodniczy
nausea mdłości
near niedaleko
nearby niedaleko
near-sighted krótkowidz
necessary konieczny
neck (body) szyja
necklace naszyjnik
need *v* potrzebować

nerve nerw

nervous system układ nerwowy

never nigdy

new nowy

newsagent [BE] kiosk z gazetami

newspaper gazeta

newsstand kiosk z gazetami

next następny

nice miły

night noc

night club klub nocny

no nie

noisy hałaśliwy

none żaden

nonsense bzdura

non-smoking *adj* dla niepalących

noon południe

normal normalny

north północ

nose nos

nothing nic

notify zawiadomić

now teraz

number numer

nurse pielęgniarka

nylon nylon

O

occasionally czasami

occupied zajęty

office (place) biuro

off-licence [BE] sklep monopolowy

often często

okay okay

old stary

old town stare miasto

on (day, date) w

once raz

one jeden

one-way w jedną stonę

one-way ticket bilet w jedną stronę

open *adj* otwarty; *v* otwierać

opening hours godziny otwarcia

opera opera

opera house opera

operation operacja

opposite naprzeciwko

optician optyk

or albo

orange (color) pomarańczowy

order *n* zamówienie; *v* zamówić

our(s) nasz

outdoor pool basen otwarty

outrageous (price) horrendalny

outside na zewnątrz

oval owalny

oven piekarnik

overcharge *v* policzyć za dużo

overheat przegrzać się

overnight na noc

owe być dłużnym
own *adj* własny
owner właściciel

P

p.m. po południu
pacifier smoczek
pack pakować
package przesyłka
paddling pool [BE] brodzik
padlock kłódka
pail (toy) wiaderko
pain ból
painkiller środek
  przeciwbólowy
paint *v* malować
painter malarz
painting obraz
pair para
palace pałac
panorama panorama
pants spodnie
pantyhose rajstopy
paper napkin serwetka
  papierowa
paper towel ręcznik
  papierowy
paracetamol [BE]
  paracetamol
paralysis paraliż
parcel [BE] paczka
parent rodzic
park *n* park; *v* parkować
parking garage parking
  podziemny

parking lot parking
parking meter parkometr
parliament building
  budynek parlamentu
partner partner
party (social) przyjęcie
passenger pasażer
passport paszport
passport number numer
  paszportu
password hasło
pastry shop sklep
  cukierniczy
patch załatać
patient *n* pacjent
pavement [BE] chodnik
pay płacić
pay phone automat
  telefoniczny
payment zapłata
peak szczyt
pearl perła
pedestrian pieszy
pedestrian crossing
  przejście dla pieszych
pedestrian zone strefa
  zamknięta dla ruchu
  kołowego
peg [BE] spinacz do bielizny
pen długopis
per za
perhaps być może
period (time) okres;
  (menstrual) miesiączka
person osoba

petrol [BE] benzyna
petrol station [BE] stacja benzynowa
pewter cyna
pharmacy apteka
phone *n* telefon; *v* dzwonić
phone card karta telefoniczna
photo zdjęcie
photocopier kopiarka
photograph zdjęcie
photographer fotograf
phrase zwrot
phrase book rozmówki
pick up odebrać
picnic piknik
picnic area miejsce piknikowe
piece (item) sztuka; (amount) kawałek
pill (contraceptive) pigułka antykoncepcyjna; (tablet) tabletka
pillow poduszka
pillow case poszewka na poduszkę
pink różowy
pipe (smoking) fajka
pitch (camping) pole namiotowe
pizzeria pizzeria
place miejsce
plan *n* plan; *v* planować
plane samolot
plant (greenery) roślina
plaster [BE] plaster

plastic *adj* plastikowy
plastic bag torebka plastikowa
plastic wrap folia spożywcza
plate talerz
platform peron; [BE] tor
platinum platyna
play *n* (theater) sztuka; *v* grać
playground plac zabaw
playing field boisko
pleasant przyjemny
please proszę
plug zatyczka
plunger przepychacz
pneumonia zapalenie płuc
point wskazać
poison trucizna
Poland Polska
police policja
police report raport policyjny
police station komisariat policji
Polish *adj* polski; *n* Polak
pollen count stężenie pyłków w powietrzu
polyester poliester
pond staw
pop (music) pop
popular popularny; (well-known) znany
port (harbor) port
porter bagażowy
portion porcja
possible możliwy

post [BE] n **(mail)** poczta; v wysłać
post office poczta
postage opłata
postcard pocztówka
poster plakat
pot (for cooking) garnek; **(for tea)** dzbanek
pottery ceramika
pound (sterling) funt
powdery (snow) puszysty
power (electricity) prąd
precipice przepaść
pregnant w ciąży
prescribe przepisać
prescription recepta
present (gift) prezent
press naciskać
pretty ładny
price cena
print n sztych; v drukować
prison więzienie
produce store sklep spożywczy
profession zawód
program program
pronounce wymawiać
pub pub
public n publiczność; adj publiczny
pump (gas station) pompa
puncture przebicie
pure czysty
purple fioletowy
purse torebka

push-chair [BE] wózek spacerowy
put włożyć

Q

quality jakość
quarter ćwierć; **(time)** kwadrans
queue [BE] n kolejka; v stać w kolejce
quick szybki
quickly szybko
quiet cichy

R

race course [BE] tor wyścigowy
racetrack tor wyścigowy
racket (tennis, squash) rakieta
railway station [BE] stacja kolejowa
rain n deszcz
raincoat płaszcz przeciwdeszczowy
rape n gwałt; v zgwałcić
rapids progi rzeczne
rare (unusual) rzadki
rash wysypka
razor maszynka do golenia
razor blade żyletka
read v czytać
ready gotowy
real (genuine) prawdziwy
rear tylny

receipt paragon
receive odebrać
reception (desk) recepcja
receptionist recepcjonista
recommend polecić
red czerwony
reduction (price) obniżka
refrigerator lodówka
refund zwrot pieniędzy
region (area) region
registered mail list polecony
registration form formularz rejestracji
reliable niezawodny
religion religia
remember pamiętać
rent wynająć
rental car wynajęty samochód
repair n naprawa; v naprawić
repeat powtórzyć
replacement wymiana
replacement part część zamienna
report (crime) zgłosić
require wymagać
reservation rezerwacja
reservations desk okienko rezerwacji
reserve v rezerwować
rest v odpoczywać
restaurant restauracja
restroom toaleta
return wrócić; (surrender) zwrócić
return ticket [BE] bilet powrotny
reverse-charge call [BE] rozmowa na koszt rozmówcy
rheumatism reumatyzm
rib żebro
right (correct) poprawny; (good) dobry
right of way pierwszeństwo przejazdu
ring pierścionek
river rzeka
road droga
road map mapa drogowa
road sign znak drogowy
rob obrabować
robbery rabunek
rock (music) rock; (land formation) skała
romantic romantyczny
roof dach
roof-rack bagażnik dachowy
room (hotel) pokój
room service room service
rope lina
round okrągły
round-trip ticket bilet powrotny
route trasa
rubbish [BE] śmieci
rude niegrzeczny
ruins ruiny

S

safe adj bezpieczny; n sejf
safety bezpieczeństwo

safety pin agrafka
sand piasek
sandal sandał
sanitary napkin podpaska
sanitary pad [BE] podpaska
satellite TV telewizja
   satelitarna
satin satyna
saucepan rondel
sauna sauna
say v powiedzieć
scarf szalik
scissors nożyczki
Scotland Szkocja
screwdriver śrubokręt
sea morze
seasickness choroba moska
season ticket bilet okresowy
seat (train) miejsce
seat reservation (train)
   miejscówka
second class druga klasa
secondhand store sklep z
   używaną odzieżą
secretary sekretarka
sedative środek uspokajający
see (spot) zobaczyć; **(inspect)**
   sprawdzić; **(observe,
   witness)** widzieć
self-employed
   samozatrudniony
self-service (gas station)
   samoobsługa
sell sprzedawać
send wysłać

senior citizen emeryt
separated w separacji
separately osobno
serious poważny
service (in restaurant)
   obsługa; **(religious)**
   nabożeństwo
sex seks; **(gender)** płeć
shade odcień
shady cienisty
shallow płytki
shampoo szampon
share v dzielić
sharp ostry
shaving cream krem do
   golenia
she ona
sheet (bed) prześcieradło
shirt (men's) koszula;
   (women's) bluzka
shock (electric) porażenie
shoe but
shoe repair naprawa obuwia
shoe store sklep z obuwiem
shop assistant sprzedawca
shopping area centrum
   handlowe
shopping basket koszyk
shopping cart wózek
shopping centre [BE] centrum
   handlowe
shopping mall centrum
   handlowe
shopping trolley [BE] wózek
short adj **(length)** krótki;

(person) niski
shorts (clothing) szorty
short-sighted [BE] krótkowidz
shoulder bark
shovel (toy) łopatka
show n **(presentation)** pokaz; **(theater)** sztuka; v pokazać
shower prysznic
shrine kapliczka
shut v zamykać; adj zamknięty
shutter okiennica
side (head) bok
side order dodatek
side street boczna uliczka
sidewalk chodnik
sights atrakcje turystyczne
sightseeing tour wycieczka po mieście
sign znak
silk jedwab
silver srebro
singer pieśniarz
single sam
single room pokój jednoosobowy
single ticket bilet w jedną stronę
sink zlew
sir pan
sister siostra
sit siadać
size rozmiar
skate łyżwa
skewer rożen
ski narta

ski boot but narciarski
ski pole kijek
skin skóra
skirt spódnica
sleep spać
sleeper car [BE] wagon sypialny
sleeping bag śpiwór
sleeping car wagon sypialny
sleeping pill tabletka nasenna
sleeve rękaw
slice plasterek
slip v poślizgnąć się
slipper pantofel
slow wolny
slowly wolno
small mały
smell pachnieć
smoke palić
smoking (area) dla palących
snack przekąska
snack bar bar
sneaker tenisówka
snorkel fajka do nurkowania
snow śnieg
soap mydło
soccer piłka nożna
sock skarpetka
socket gniazdko
sole (shoes) podeszwa
some jakiś
something coś
sometimes czasami
somewhere gdzieś
son syn

soon niedługo

sore throat ból gardła

sorry przepraszam

soul (music) soul

sour kwaśne

south południe

souvenir pamiątka

souvenir store sklep z pamiątkami

spa spa

space miejsce

spare zapasowy

speak mówić

special specjalny

specialist specjalista

specimen próbka

spell v przeliterować

spend (time) spędzać; (money) wydawać

spicy ostry

sponge gąbka

spoon łyżka

sport sport

sporting goods store sklep sportowy

spot (place, site) miejsce

sprained skręcony

spring wiosna

square kwadrat

stadium stadion

staff personel

stain plama

stainless steel stal nierdzewna

stairs schody

stamp (postal) znaczek

standby ticket tani bilet okazyjny

start v (begin) zaczynać się; (car) zapalić

starter [BE] przekąska

statement (police) zeznanie

stationery store sklep papierniczy

statue pomnik

stay n pobyt; v zostać; (in a hotel) zatrzymać się

sterilizing solution płyn do sterylizacji

still adv wciąż

stockings [BE] pończochy

stolen ukradziony

stomach brzuch

stomachache ból brzucha

stop n (bus, tram) przystanek; v zatrzymywać się

store sklep

store guide tablica informacyjna

storm burza

stove kuchenka

strange dziwny

straw (drinking) słomka

stream strumień

strong (powerful) silny

student student

study v studiować

style styl

subtitled z napisami

suggest zasugerować
suit (men's) garnitur;
(women's) kostium
suitable stosowny
suitcase walizka
summer lato
sunbathe opalać się
sunburn oparzenie słoneczne
sunglasses okulary słoneczne
sunny słoneczny
sunshade parasol
sunstroke udar słoneczny
suntan lotion krem do
opalania
superb znakomity
supermarket supermarket
supervision nadzór
supplement opłata dodatkowa
suppository czopek
sure pewien
surfboard deska do
serfowania
surname nazwisko
sweater sweter
sweatshirt bluza
sweet (taste) słodki
swelling opuchlizna
swim pływać
swimming pool basen
swimming trunks kąpielówki
swimsuit kostium kąpielowy
swollen spuchnięty
symptom (illness) objaw
synagogue synagoga

T

table stolik
take brać; (carry) zanieść;
(medicine) brać; (time)
trwać
take away [BE] na wynos
talk rozmawiać
tall wysoki
tampon tampon
tan opalenizna
tap [BE] kran
tapestry kilim
taxi taksówka
taxi rank [BE] postój
taksówek
taxi stand postój taksówek
teacher nauczyciel
team drużyna
teaspoon łyżeczka do
herbaty
teddy bear miś
telephone n telefon; v
dzwonić
telephone bill rachunek
telefoniczny
telephone booth budka
telefoniczna
telephone call rozmowa
telefoniczna
telephone number numer
telefonu
tell powiedzieć
temperature temperatura
temple świątynia

temporarily tymczasowo

tennis tenis

tennis court kort tenisowy

tent namiot

tent peg kołek

tent pole maszt namiotowy

terminal terminal

terrace taras

terrible okropny

terrific wspaniały

tetanus tężec

text *n* (phone) sms; (document) tekst

thank *v* dziękować

thank you dziękuję

that to

theater teatr

theft kradzież

their(s) ich

theme park tematyczny park rozrywki

then (time) wtedy

there tam

thermometer termometr

these ci

they oni

thick gruby

thief złodziej

thigh udo

thin chudy

think myśleć

thirsty spragniony

this (one) ten

those tamci

thousand tysiąc

throat gardło

through przez

thumb kciuk

ticket bilet

ticket office kasa biletowa

tie krawat

tight *adv* ciasny

tights (clothing) rajstopy

time czas; (exact time) godzina

timetable [BE] rozkład jazdy

tin opener [BE] otwieracz do puszek

tire (car) opona

tired zmęczony

tissue chusteczka

to do

tobacco tytoń

tobacconist sklep tytoniowy

today dzisiaj

toe palec u nogi

toilet [BE] toaleta

toilet paper papier toaletowy

tomorrow jutro

tongue język

tonight dziś wieczorem

too (extreme) za

tooth ząb

toothache ból zęba

toothbrush szczoteczka do zębów

toothpaste pasta do zębów

top (head) góra

torn naderwany

tour wycieczka

tour guide przewodnik wycieczki

tour operator organizator wycieczki

tourist turysta

tourist office biuro informacji turystycznej

tow truck pomoc drogowa

towel ręcznik

tower wieża

town miasto

town center centrum

town hall ratusz

toy zabawka

track tor

traditional tradycyjny

traffic ruch

traffic jam korek

traffic light światła

traffic violation wykroczenie drogowe

trailer przyczepa

train pociąg

train station dworzec kolejowy

trained wykwalifikowany

tram tramwaj

transit (travel) przejazd

translate tłumaczyć

translation tłumaczenie

translator tłumacz

trash (garbage) śmieci

trash can śmietnik

travel n podróż; v podróżować

travel agency biuro podróży

travelers check czek podróżny

travelers cheque [BE] czek podróżny

tray taca

tree drzewo

trim v podstrzyc

trip wycieczka

trolley wózek

trousers spodnie

truck ciężarówka

true prawdziwy

try próbować

try on (clothes) przymierzyć

T-shirt t-shirt

tumor nowotwór

tunnel tunel

turn skręcić

turn down zmniejszyć

turn off wyłączyć

turn on włączyć

turn up (volume, heat) zwiększyć

TV telewizor

tweezers pinceta

twice dwa razy

twin bed łóżko podwójne

twist v (hurt) skręcić

type (sort) rodzaj

typical typowy

tyre [BE] opona

U

U.K. Wielka Brytania

U.S. Stany Zjednoczone

ugly brzydki

ulcer wrzód

umbrella parasol
uncle wuj
uncomfortable niewygodny
unconscious nieprzytomny
under pod
understand rozumieć
underwear bielizna
undress rozbierać (się)
uneven (ground) nierówny
unfortunately niestety
uniform mundur
unit (phone card) impuls
university uniwersytet
unleaded (gas)
  bezołowiowa
unlimited mileage bez
  limitu kilometrów
unlock otworzyć
unpleasant niemiły
unscrew odkręcić
urgent pilny

V

vacation wakacje
vacuum cleaner odkurzacz

vegetarian *adj*
  wegetariański; *n*
  wegetarianin
visa wiza

W

wait czekać
wallet portfel
water woda
week tydzień
where gdzie
white biały
window okno
window seat siedzenie przy
  oknie
wine list lista win
wireless bezprzewodowy
work *v* **(function)** działać;
  (job) pracować

X

X-ray rentgen

POLISH–ENGLISH

A

à droite right (direction)
aktualny up-to-date
alarm przeciwpożarowy fire alarm
aleja boulevard
ambasada embassy
angielski English
Anglia England
antyki antiques store
aparat fotograficzny camera
apteka pharmacy
artykuły bezcłowe duty-free goods
aseptyczny antiseptic
astma asthma
atrakcja turystyczna tourist attraction
autokar long-distance bus [coach BE]
autostrada highway [motorway BE]

B

bagaż baggage
bagaż podręczny carry-on [hand luggage BE]
bagno marsh
balkon balcony (theater)
balsam po opalaniu after-sun lotion
bankomat ATM

basen dla dzieci children's pool
basen kryty indoor swimming pool
basen odkryty outdoor swimming pool
benzyna gas [petrol BE]
bez cukru sugar-free
bez tłuszczu fat-free
bezglutenowy gluten-free
bezołowiowy unleaded (gasoline)
bezprzewodowy wireless (internet)
bezzwrotny non-returnable
biblioteka library
biegać v run
biegówki cross-coutry skis
bielizna underwear
bilet ticket
bilet elektroniczny e-ticket
bilet grupowy group ticket
bilet okresowy season ticket
bilet parkingowy parking ticket
biuro office
biuro obsługi klienta customer service
biuro podróży travel agency
biuro rzeczy znalezionych lost-and-found [lost-property office BE]

biuro turystyczne tourist office

biznes business

biżuteria jewelry

błąd mistake

blokada lock (on a bike)

błyszczyk lipgloss

ból pain

budka autobusowa bus shelter

bungalow bungalow

but shoe

butelka bottle

C

cena price

centrum biznesu business district

centrum handlowe shopping mall [centre BE]

centrum miasta downtown area [town centre BE]

centrum odnowy biologicznej spa

centrum ogrodnicze garden center

chemiczna toaleta chemical toilet

chodnik sidewalk [pavement BE]

ciepły warm (water)

ciężarówka truck

ciężki heavy (luggage)

cło duty (customs)

cmentarz cemetery

cukiernia pastry shop

czasopismo magazine

czek check [cheque BE]

czek podróżny travelers check [cheque BE]

czekać wait

D

dabingowany dubbed

dania dnia menu of the day

darowizna donation

data urodzenia date of birth

data ważności expiration [expiry BE] date

dawkowanie dosage

deklaracja celna customs declaration

delikatesy delicatessen

deska do windsurfingu windsurfing board

deska surfingowa surfboard

dieta diet

długopis pen

do until

do wynajęcia for rent [hire BE]

do żucia chewable (tablets)

dokładna reszta exact change

dom mieszkalny apartment building

dom towarowy department store

domowej roboty homemade

dostawa delivery

dostęp access

dowód tożsamości

identification
dozorca caretaker
drewno wood
droga road
drzewo tree
drzwi automatyczne automatic doors
drzwi przeciwpożarowe fire door
dworzec autobusowy bus station
dworzec kolejowy train station
dzbanek pot (for tea)
działać v work
działanie uboczne side effect
dziecko child
dzień day
dzień powszedni weekday
dzisiaj today

E

e-mail e-mail
emeryt senior citizen
epilepsja epilepsy
epileptyk epileptic

F

fabryka factory
fajerwerk firework
faks fax
festyn fair
filharmonia concert hall
filiżanka cup

folia aluminiowa aluminum [kitchen BE] foil
formularz form
fotelik dziecięcy car seat
fryzjer hairdresser
funt pound (sterling)

G

gabinet dentystyczny dental office [surgery BE]
gabinet lekarski doctor's office [surgery BE]
galeria gallery
garnek pot (for cooking)
gaśnica fire extinguisher
gdzie where
giełda stock exchange
głęboko deep
godzina hour
godziny urzędowania business hours
godziny wizyt visiting hours
góra mountain
gorączka temperature
gość guest
gospodarstwo farm
gotować v boil
gotówka cash

H

hala targowa indoor market
hamulec bezpieczeństwa emergency brake
hasło password

I

ile how many, how much
imię name
informacja information desk
informacja dla klientów customer information
informacja o lotach flight information
informacja o sklepie store directory [guide BE]
instruktor instructor
internet internet
izba przyjęć emergency ward

J

jadalnia dining room
jakość quality
jaskinia cave
jasny light (color)
jeden one
jedwab silk
jedzenie na wynos to go [take-away BE] (food)
jesień fall [autumn BE]
jeść eat
jezioro lake
jeździectwo horseback riding
język tongue (part of body); language
język obcy foreign language
jubiler jeweler
jutro tomorrow

K

kafejka internetowa internet cafe
kamizelka ratunkowa life jacket
kantor currency exchange office
kapliczka shrine
kapsułka capsule (medication)
karetka ambulance
karta key card (hotel)
karta do telefonu phone card
karta kredytowa credit card
karta pokładowa boarding pass (airport)
karta rabatowa discount card
karta win wine list
kasa biletowa ticket office
kasa ekspresowa express checkout
kasjer cashier
kask crash helmet
katedra cathedral
kaucja deposit
kawałek piece
klieliszek glass (alcoholic)
kierownik manager
kierunek direction (map)
kilometr kilometer
kiosk z gazetami newsstand
klasa biznes business class
klasa turystyczna economy class
klif cliff

klimatyzacja air conditioning
klimatyzator air conditioner
klinika clinic
kolejka linowa cable car
koło ratunkowe life preserver [belt BE]
komiks comic book
komisariat police station
kompresor air pump (gas station)
komputer computer
koncert concert
konkurs contest
kontaktować v contact
kontrola celna customs control
kontroler biletów ticket inspector
korek traffic jam
kościół church
kosmetyki cosmetics
koszerny kosher
kosztować v cost
koszyk shopping basket
kradzież theft
krajowy domestic (flight)
kran faucet [tap BE]
krem nawilżający moisturizer
krem z blokadą UV sunscreen
kropla drop (medication)
krwotok bleeding
książka telefoniczna directory

księgarnia bookstore
kucharz cook, chef
kuchenka mikrofalowa microwave
kuchnia kitchen
kurs wymiany exchange rate
kuszetka berth (train)
kwiaciarnia florist
kwiat flower
kwota amount (money)

L

lądować arrive (plane)
las forest
latarnia morska lighthouse
lato summer
lecieć v fly
lekarz doctor
lekki light (weight)
leżak deck chair
linia (lotnicza) airline
list polecony registered letter
list priorytetowy express mail
lista drinków drink menu
lokalny local
lot flight
loteria lottery
lotnisko airport
lotnisko krajowe domestic airport
lotnisko międzynarodowe international airport
lubić v like

Ł

łazienka bathroom
łopatka spatula
łódź ratunkowa life boat
łóżeczko dziecięce crib
  [child's cot *BE*]
łóżko bed
łyżka do odmierzania
  measuring spoon
łyżwiarstwo ice skating
łyżwy ice skates

M

mały small (size)
mapa drogowa road map
matka mother
mdłości nausea
mdły bland
meble furniture
mgła fog
miarka kuchenna measuring
  cup
miejsce seat (bus, train,
  plane)
miejsce na piknik picnic area
miejsce przy oknie window
  seat
miejsce przy przejściu aisle
  seat
miejsce urodzenia place of
  birth
miejsce zbiórki meeting place
  [point *BE*]
miejscówka reservation (train)

międzynarodowy international
mikrofalówka mircowave
miska bowl
mleczarnia dairy
młodzież youth
młyn windmill
mniej less
moczary swamp
mokry wet
mop mop
morze sea
motor motorcycle
motorower moped
mówić speak
msza mass
muzeum museum
mydło soap

N

na dole downstairs
na górze upstairs
na zewnątrz outside
nadbagaż excess baggage
namiot tent
napad mugging
napisać write
napiwek tip
naprawa *n* repair (car)
naprawić *v* fix (a car)
narty wodne water skis
następny next
nawierzchnia road surface
nawilżacz moisturizer
nazwisko last name
nazwisko panieńskie maiden

name

niedaleko close

niepalący non-smoking

nierówny uneven (surface)

noc night

nocleg accommodation

nocny dyżur night duty

nocny portier night porter

normalny normal

nowy new

numer kierunkowy country code

numer lotu flight number

numer miejsca seat number

numer pierwszej pomocy emergency number

O

objazd detour [diversion *BE*]

obóz *n* camp

obozować *v* camp

od from (time)

odbiór bagażu baggage claim

oddział department

odebrać receive

odkurzacz vacuum cleaner

odlatywać leave

odprawa check-in (airport)

odprawa bagażu baggage check

odwołany cancelled

odzież damska ladieswear

odzież męska menswear

ognisko campfire

ograniczenie prędkości speed limit

ogród garden

okazja bargain

okno window

okres period (of time); menstruation

okulary glasses (optical)

okulary przeciwsłoneczne sunglasses

opera opera

opis description

opłata bankowa bank charge

opłata obowiązkowa minimum charge **opłata za dzień** day charge

opłata za usługę service charge

opłata za wstęp admission charge

opóźniony delayed

optyk optician

ostry spicy

ostrzeżenie warning

otwarty open (shop)

P

paczka package [parcel *BE*]

paczka ekspresowa express mail

pakować pack

palacz smoker

paliwo fuel

pan sir

pani madam

panie ladies (toilet)

panna miss
panowie gentlemen (toilet)
papierowy ręcznik paper towel
paragon receipt
parasol umbrella [sunshade BE]
park narodowy national park
park publiczny public park
parking parking lot [car park BE]
parking podziemny underground garage
parking wielopoziomowy parking garage
parkometr parking meter
parkować v park
parter first floor [ground floor BE]; orchestra [stalls BE] (theater)
pas lane
pasażer passenger
pasmo górskie mountain range
pawilon pavilion
pchać push
pchli targ flea market
peron platform
piasek sand
pić v drink
piekarnia bakery
pielęgniarka nurse
pieniądze money
pierwsza klasa first class
pierwsza pomoc emergency services; first aid
pierwsze piętro second floor [first floor BE]
pieszy pedestrian
piętro floor (level in building)
pigułka pill
pikantny spicy
pilny urgent
pismo periodical
piwnica basement
plac square
plasterek slice
plaża dla nudystów nudist beach
plecak backpack
plomba filling (dental)
płacić v pay
płeć sex (gender)
płyta kompaktowa CD
płytki adj shallow
pływać v swim
po południu p.m.
pociąg Intercity Intercity train
pociąg lokalny local train
początkujący beginner
poczekalnia waiting room
poczta post office
podarunek gift
podjazd ramp
podłoga floor
podobać się like
podpaska sanitary napkin [pad BE]
podróż powrotna round-trip [return trip BE] (ticket)

poduszka pillow
pokład deck (ship)
pokoje do wynajęcia rooms for rent [to let BE]
pokój room (hotel)
pole field
pole bitwy battle site
pole namiotowe camping
polecać recommend
policja police
policja drogowa traffic police
polisa ubezpieczeniowa insurance card [certificate BE]
Polska Poland
południe noon (time); south (direction)
pomiędzy between
pomnik monument
pomoc drogowa breakdown services
poranek morning
port port
portfel wallet
postój taksówek taxi stand [rank BE]
pościel sheets
potrzebny required
potwierdzenie confirmation
potwierdzić confirm
powiedzieć v say
powtórzyć repeat
poznać meet
pożar fire
północ midnight (time); north (direction)

półwysep peninsula
pracować v work
prać oddzielnie wash separately
prać ręcznie hand wash only
pralnia laundry
pralnia chemiczna dry-cleaner
prasować v iron
prawnik lawyer
prawo jazdy driver's license
priorytet express mail
progi rzeczne rapids
prognoza pogody weather forecast
prom ferry
proszę please
prowizja commission
prysznic shower
prywatny private
przebieralnia fitting room
przecena sale
przechowalnia bagażu baggage office
przeciek leak
przed before
przed południem a.m.
przedstawić introduce (someone)
przedział compartment
przejście path; aisle (plane)
przejście dla pieszych pedestrian crossing
przejście podziemne

underpass
przejściówka adapter
przekaz pieniężny money order
przekąska appetizer [starter BE]
przepaść precipice
przepychacz plunger
przesiadać się change [transfer BE] (bus)
przesyłka package
przeszkadzać disturb
przetłumaczyć translate
przewodnik guide (person); guidebook
przyczepa trailer
przyloty arrivals (airport)
przymierzalnia fitting room
przystanek autobusowy bus stop
przystanek na żądanie on-demand stop
ptak bird
punkt widzenia view point
pusty vacant

R

rabat discount
ratownik lifeguard
ratusz town hall
recepta prescription
recycling recycling
ręcznie robione handmade
ręcznik towel
rejs cruise

reklama advertisment
rentgen X-ray
restauracja restaurant
reszta n change (money)
rezerwacja reservation
rezerwuar reservoir
robak bug
rogatka toll booth
rondel saucepan
rondo roundabout
room service room service
rower bicycle
rozkład jazdy schedule [timetable BE]
rozkładane łóżko cot
rozmowa na koszt rozmówcy collect call [reverse-charge call BE]
rozumieć understand
rura pipe (water)
rząd row (of seats, people)
rzeka river
rzeźnik butcher

S

sąd courthouse
sala hall (large public room)
sala konferencyjna conference room
sala zebrań convention hall
salon gier arcade
sam alone
samolot plane
sauna sauna
schowek na bagaż luggage

locker

schronisko młodzieżowe youth hostel

ściana wall

ścieżka path

sekretarka secretary

serwetka napkin

sieć network (of computers); chain (of stores)

siedzenie seat

siedzenie przy korytarzu aisle seat

siedzenie przy oknie window seat

silnik engine

siłownia gym

skala scale

skała rock

skasować validate (ticket)

skipass ski pass

sklep store

sklep bezcłowy duty-free store

sklep mięsny butcher shop

sklep muzyczny music store

sklep osiedlowy convenience store

sklep papierniczy stationery store

sklep z narzędziami hardware store

sklep z zabawkami toy store

sklep ze zdrową żywnością health food store

skóra leather; skin

skręcić v turn

skrytka bagażowa luggage locker

skrzynka pocztowa mailbox [postbox BE]

skrzyżowanie intersection [junction BE]

skuter wodny jet-ski

ślepy zaułek dead end

śliski slippery

słony salty

śmieci trash [rubbish BE]

śniadanie breakfast

spa spa

śpiący policjant speed bump

spotkanie appointment (business); meeting (friends)

spóźniony late

stacja benzynowa gas [petrol BE] station

stacja kolejowa train [railway BE] station

stadion stadium

stal steel

stanowisko odprawy check-in desk (airport)

Stany Zjednoczone United States

startować take off, depart

statek ship

staw pond

steward flight attendant

stój codzienny casual clothing

stolik table

straż pożarna fire station

strażak firefighter

strój suit, clothing

strój wieczorowy evening dress

strój wizytowy formal dress

strumień stream

studiować *v* study

suszarka do włosów hairdryer

światła traffic light

światło light

święto państwowe national holiday

świeży fresh

szewc shoe repair [cobbler *BE*]

szklanka glass (non-alcoholic)

szkoła school

szlak trail

szpital hospital

T

tabletka tablet

taksówka taxi

talerz plate

targ market

telefon phone

telefon komórkowy cell phone [mobile phone *BE*]

telefon publiczny pay phone

telefonistka operator (phone)

terminal terminal

toaleta restroom [toilet *BE*]

tor track [platform *BE*]

tor wyścigowy racetrack [race course *BE*]

torebka purse [handbag *BE*]

trampolina diving board

trasa route

trasa autobusowa bus route

trawa grass

turystyka piesza hiking

tutaj here

tydzień week

tylko only

U

ubezpieczenie insurance

ugryzienie bite

ulepszony improved

ulica street

ulica jednokierunkowa one-way street

uniwersytet university

unowocześniony modernized

usługa service

uwaga attention

W

w budowie under construction

w jedną stronę one-way (trip)

wagon car (train)

wagon restauracyjny dining car (train)

wakacyjny rozkład jazdy holiday schedule [timetable *BE*]

walizka suitcase

waluta obca foreign currency

warsztat samochodowy car mechanic [repair garage *BE*]

wąwóz gorge

wejście entrance; gate (at the airport)

wełna wool

wentylator fan (electric)

wesołe miasteczko amusement park

wewnętrzny extension (phone)

wiadomość news

widelec fork

więcej more

Wielka Brytania Great Britain

wieczór evening

wiedza knowledge

winda elevator [lift *BE*]

windsurfing windsurfing

wiosna spring

włączyć turn on

własność prywatna private property

woda water

wolno slowly

wolny free (place)

wolny pokój vacancy (accommodation)

wózek bagażowy luggage cart [trolley *BE*]

wpłata deposit

wschód east

wskazówka instruction

wspinaczka rock climbing

wstęp wolny admission free

wstęp wzbroniony no access

wybrzeże coast

wydarzenie event

wydrukować *v* print

wyjście exit; gate (at the airport)

wyjście bezpieczeństwa emergency exit

wyjście przeciwpożarowe fire exit

wyjście wzbronione no exit

wykręcić dial

wyłączyć turn off

wylogować się log off

wymiana exchange

wymiana walut currency exchange

wynajem samochodów car rental [hire *BE*]

wypadek accident

wypłata cash withdrawal

wyprzedaż clearance

wyprzedzać *v* pass (car)

wysiąść get off (bus, train)

wysłać send

wysokie krzesełko highchair

występ show (in front of audience)

wzbroniony forbidden

wzgórze hill

Z

z napisami subtitled

zaawansowany advanced

zabawka toy

zachód west

zaczekać wait

zadzwonić call (phone)

zagraniczny international (flight); foreign (product)

zajazd guest house

zakaźny contagious, infectious

zakupy shopping

zalogować się log on

zamawiać v order

zamek castle (building); lock (door)

zamknięty closed (store)

zamówienie n order

zamrożony frozen

zamykać v lock

zapakować wrap

zapakować na prezent giftwrap

zaparcie constipation

zapinać fasten (seat belt)

zapłacony paid

zapominać forget

zarezerwować reserve (tickets)

zatkany blocked

zatłoczony crowded

zatoka bay

zatrzymać się stay (at a hotel); stop (not move)

zebra pedestrian crossing

zepsuty broken

zgwałcić v rape

zima winter

zimno adv cold

zimny adj cold

złoto gold

zły bad

znaczek stamp

znaczek pocztowy postage stamp

znaczyć mean (meaning)

znak drogowy road sign

zniżka discount

zwolnić slow down

zwrot pieniędzy refund

zwrotny returnable

Ż

żelazko n iron